DATE DUE

MAR 1 4 2017		
DISCARD		

Taking Flight

Taking Flight

•◦• From War Orphan to Star Ballerina •◦•

MICHAELA DEPRINCE

with ELAINE DEPRINCE

ALFRED A. KNOPF 🐎 NEW YORK

THIS IS A BORZOI BOOK PUBLISHED BY ALFRED A. KNOPF

Visit us on the Web! randomhouseteens.com

Educators and librarians, for a variety of teaching tools, visit us at
RHTeachersLibrarians.com

Library of Congress Cataloging-in-Publication Data
DePrince, Michaela
Taking flight : from war orphan to star ballerina / Michaela DePrince,
Elaine DePrince.
p. cm.
Summary: "The memoir of Michaela DePrince, who lived the first few years
of her life in war-torn Sierra Leone until being adopted by an American family.
Now seventeen, she is one of the premier ballerinas in the United States."
—Provided by publisher
ISBN 978-0-385-75511-5 (trade) — ISBN 978-0-385-75512-2 (lib. bdg.) —
ISBN 978-0-385-75513-9 (ebook)
1. DePrince, Michaela. 2. Ballet dancers—Sierra Leone—Biography—Juvenile
literature. 3. Ballet dancers—United States—Biography—Juvenile literature.
I. DePrince, Elaine. II. Title.
GV1785.D37A3 2014
792.802'8092—dc23
[B]
2013048188

The text of this book is set in 11.5-point Berling.

Printed in the United States of America
October 2014
10 9 8 7 6

First Edition

To Charles DePrince,
gentle and generous father and husband

THE BLACK SWAN

I stand in the wings, dressed in a lush black tutu embellished with black feathers and blood-red flowers. A silver tiara studded with crystal rhinestones crowns my hair, which is pulled tightly back in a thick bun. One at a time I flex my feet at the ankles, extend my legs, and point my toes to check that the ribbons of my pointe shoes are tied and securely tucked. "A professional ballerina never allows her ribbons to flop loose around her ankles," one of my favorite teachers used to warn me. A tiny smile twitches at the corners of my mouth as I remember that seven-year-old girl with her ribbons flying about.

A sense of unreality grips me. A professional ballerina . . . is that really me? It seems that just yesterday I was an orphan child, a small, dirty-faced pikin—hungry, frightened, and clinging for dear life to a dream of becoming a ballerina. As Mabinty Bangura, I danced on my bare toes in the mud of the rainy season, disturbing the breeding mosquitoes, who would rise up in anger and bite me—bringing malaria.

My arms prickle with goose bumps. I rub them away, remembering my sister Mia once telling me, "They're swan bumps, Michaela, not goose bumps." Are my swan bumps caused by nervousness, the chilly Berkshire air in the Ted Shawn Theatre at Jacob's Pillow, or haunting memories?

Why should I be nervous? This isn't the first time I've danced the act-two pas de deux from *Swan Lake* onstage as Odile, the dark and cunning daughter of the evil sorcerer Von Rothbart. But it is the first time I have danced it in front of such a large audience of critics and other dancers. They flock to Jacob's Pillow in June of each year to attend this renowned festival, and here I am about to make my entrance, the youngest professional ballerina among them, dancing a role that demands maturity and sophistication. I feel like an imposter.

The Black Swan is a seductress, tantalizing Prince Siegfried with her womanly charms in order to steal him away from Odette, the White Swan. What do I know about womanly charms or seduction? After my April performance, one critic wrote, "She was the sweetest seductress you ever saw . . . but she has yet to develop any ballerina mystique. She is only eighteen." I showed the review to

Skyler, my boyfriend. "Do you agree?" I asked him, with tears in my eyes.

"She's right. You are sweet," he answered.

"But I don't want to be sweet. I want to have womanly charms. I want to be a seductress. I want ballerina mystique."

Skyler laughed and said, "You're cute and funny too."

"But I don't want to be cute and funny. I want to be mysterious."

"Well, sometimes you're a complete mystery to me," he admitted with a mischievous grin.

"That's not the same as ballerina mystique."

Now it's the final performance of the season. I need to pull it off. For a brief second I am tempted to flee. Then the music starts, and I step onto the stage. Suddenly I am neither Mabinty Bangura nor Michaela DePrince. I *am* the Black Swan, and as a reviewer later acknowledges, "The vile Odile was delightfully chilly as she seduced the unwitting prince."

Chapter 1

From the House on the Right

Before I was the "vile" and "chilly" Odile, I was Michaela DePrince, and before I was Michaela, I was Mabinty Bangura, and this is the story of my flight from war orphan to ballerina.

In Africa my papa loved the dusty, dry winds of the Harmattan, which blew down from the Sahara Desert every December or January. "Ah, the Harmattan has brought us good fortune again!" he would exclaim when he returned from harvesting rice. I would smile when he said that because I knew that his next words would be "But not as good a fortune as the year when it brought us Mabinty . . . no, never as good as that!"

My parents said that I was born with a sharp cry and a personality as prickly as an African hedgehog. Even worse,

I was a girl child—and a spotted one at that, because I was born with a skin condition called vitiligo, which caused me to look like a baby leopard. Nevertheless, my parents celebrated my arrival with joy.

When my father proclaimed that my birth was the high point of his life, his older brother, Abdullah, shook his head and declared, "It is an unfortunate Harmattan that brings a girl child . . . a worthless, spotted girl child, one who will not even bring you a good bride-price." My mother told me that my father laughed at his brother. He and Uncle Abdullah did not see eye to eye on almost anything.

My uncle was right in one respect: in a typical household in the Kenema District of southeastern Sierra Leone, West Africa, my birth would not have been cause for celebration. But our household was not typical. First of all, my parents' marriage had not been arranged. They had married for love, and my father refused to take a second wife, even after several years of marriage, when it appeared that I would be their only child. Secondly, both of my parents could read, and my father believed that his daughter should learn to read as well.

"If my brother is right and no one will wish to marry a girl with skin like the leopard, it is important that our daughter go to school. Let's prepare her for that day," my father told my mother. So he began to teach me the Arabic alphabet when I was just a tiny pikin, barely able to toddle about.

"Fool!" Uncle Abdullah sputtered when he saw Papa molding my little fingers around a stick of charcoal. "Why are you teaching a girl child? She will think that she is above her station. All she needs to learn is how to cook, clean, sew, and care for children."

My spots scared the other children in our village. Nobody would play with me, except my cousins on occasion, so I would often sit alone on the stoop of our hut, thinking. I wondered why my father worked so hard panning for diamonds in the alluvial mines, diamonds that he would not be allowed to keep. It was hard, backbreaking work to stand bent over all day. Papa would hobble home at night, because his back, ankles, and feet ached. His hands would be swollen and painful from sifting the heavy, wet soil through his sieve. Then, one night while Mama was rubbing shea butter mixed with hot pepper into Papa's swollen joints, I overheard a conversation between them, and understood.

"It is important that our daughter go to school to learn more than we are capable of teaching her. I want her to go to a good school."

"If we are frugal, the money from the mines will eventually be enough to pay her school fees, Alhaji," my mother said.

"Ah, Jemi, count the money. How much have we saved so far?" Papa asked.

Mama laughed. "This much, plus the amount I counted the last time you asked," she said, holding up the coins he had brought home that evening.

I smiled a secret smile from my small space behind the curtain. I loved to listen to my parents' voices at night. Though I cannot say the same for the voices of Uncle Abdullah and his wives.

Our house was set to the right of my uncle's house. Uncle Abdullah had three wives and fourteen children. Much to his unhappiness, thirteen of his children were girls, leaving my uncle and his precious son, Usman, the child of his first wife, as the only males in the household.

Many nights I would hear cries and shouts of anger drifting across the yard. The sounds of Uncle Abdullah beating his wives and daughters filled my family with sadness. I doubted that Uncle Abdullah ever loved any of his wives, or he would not have beaten them. He certainly didn't love his many daughters. He blamed any and all of his misfortunes on their existence.

My uncle cared only about his one son. He called Usman his treasure and fed him delicious tidbits of meat while his daughters looked on, hungry and bloated from a starchy diet of rice and cassava, that long, brown-skinned root vegetable that lacks protein, vitamins, and minerals. And nothing was more galling to my uncle than finding me outside, sitting cross-legged on a grass mat, studying and writing my letters, which I copied from the Qur'an. He could not resist poking me with the toe of his sandal and ordering me to get about the duties of a woman.

"Fool!" Uncle Abdullah would sputter at my papa. "Put this child to work."

"What need does she have of womanly chores? She is only a child herself," Papa would remind his brother, and then couldn't resist adding: "Yes, not even four years old, and yet she speaks Mende, Temne, Limba, Krio, and Arabic. She picks up languages from the marketplace and learns quickly. She will surely become a scholar." Papa didn't need to rub any more salt in Uncle Abdullah's wounds by reminding him that Usman, who was several years older than me, lagged far behind me in his studies.

"What she needs is a good beating," Uncle Abdullah would counter. "And that wife of yours, she too needs an occasional beating. You are spoiling your women, Alhaji. No good will ever come of that."

Perhaps Papa should not have bragged about my learning. The villagers and my uncle thought that I was strange enough with my spots, and my reading made me even stranger in their eyes and made my uncle hate me.

The only thing that my father and his brother had in common was the land that fed us, sheltered us, and provided the rice, palm wine, and shea butter that we sold at the market.

At night, when I heard the cries coming from across

the yard, I'd turn my ear toward my parents resting on the other side of the curtain. From there I heard sweet words of love and soft laughter. Then I would thank Allah because I had been born into the house on the right, rather than the one on the left.

Chapter 2

TO THE HOUSE ON THE LEFT

A civil war had started in my country in 1991, and by the time I was three years old, it had been going on for seven years. It had begun mainly because the education system had shut down, and without schooling, young people could not get jobs. This resulted in poverty and hunger, which made them desperate, so they formed a revolutionary army to fight for what they needed.

As the war progressed, the youth lost track of their goals and started killing innocent villagers. So now, instead of good luck, the dry season brought an invasion of rebels of the Revolutionary United Front. They called themselves the RUF, but their victims combined the English words *rebel* and *devil*, and called them *debils*.

The Harmattan that my father had always loved betrayed us that year. Instead of good luck, it brought the war to our village. Papa was not at home the day the debils burned the rice and palm trees that grew on the nearby hillsides. He was at the diamond mines. When he got home, Mama would need to tell him that the debils had left us with no crop to sell, no rice to eat, and no seed for next year's planting.

Mama and I sat on a wooden bench at the front of our home and watched the flames that were being spread by the strong Harmattan winds. The smoke made it difficult to breathe. I sobbed and coughed, and she wrapped her arms around me. "Mama, why aren't you crying?" I asked.

Mama pointed toward another village on the hillside. I could see smoke rising from the homes there. "We are fortunate that the debils spared our homes and our lives," she answered. "We should be grateful to Allah for that."

Maybe she was right, but I didn't feel grateful. A few minutes later, a man came to our door, moaning and wailing. He told us that he was the only survivor of his village. The debils had forced him to watch as they killed his friends and family. Then, laughing, they asked if he preferred short sleeves or long sleeves. He said that he usually wore long sleeves, so they cut off his hand and sent him on his way to spread fear and warnings throughout the countryside.

Auntie Yeabu, the youngest wife of Uncle Abdullah, helped my mother bandage the man's stump while I stood nearby, shaking with fear. Mama offered the man the small portion of rice remaining from our morning meal. She begged him to rest in our house. But the man was certain that the debils would soon pass through our village, recognize him, and kill him too. So, instead of resting, he hurried north toward Makeni, a city many kilometers away, where he thought it might be safe.

Mama scooped less rice than usual into the cook pot that night. I knew that she would barely eat any of it, so that Papa and I could fill our bellies. I decided that I would follow her example. After working all day at the diamond mines, Papa would need the largest serving of rice.

While the rice bubbled in the pot, we continued to wait for him. Mama insisted that I eat. "I want to wait for Papa," I protested.

"No, you eat. I will wait," Mama said. "You are a growing child. Eat."

"I'm not hungry," I cried. I curled up next to her and fell asleep.

I woke up to the sound of my cousin Usman's voice. "Auntie Jemi," he hissed quietly. "Auntie Jemi, the rebels came to the mines today. They shot all of the workers."

"All of the workers?" my mother repeated. "And Alhaji?"

"Yes, Uncle Alhaji too," Usman whispered.

"NO-O-O!" I screamed. "Not Papa!"

"NO-O-O!" Mama screamed. "Not my Alhaji!"

Mama and I clung tightly to each other. She rocked me in her arms as I cried loudly.

Soon the entire village was filled with weeping, because nearly every family lost a father, brother, son, or nephew. On the day my father died, I believed that I was feeling the worst pain possible . . . that I would never again feel such pain. Then I moved into the house on the left and learned that pain, like the green of the jungle leaves, comes in many shades.

Uncle Abdullah decided to rent our house to a refugee family and forced Mama and me to move into his house. According to Sharia, Muslim law, Uncle Abdullah became our guardian. He took the money my parents had saved for my education, and because we had no money left, Mama and I could not escape. My uncle wanted to marry Mama, but Sharia also gave her the right to refuse his offer, which she did. Her rejection enraged him, and he would use any excuse to punish us.

Mama and I lived in constant fear of him. I'll never forget him shouting at us, "You are punished! No food for either of you! No food today, tomorrow, and the day after that!"

Auntie Yeabu tried to sneak food to us, but she wasn't always able to do so, because my other aunts' eyes were too sharp. We often went hungry, and for months Mama gave me most of her food. "I'm not so hungry today. You eat my rice," she would say to me. I didn't believe her, so I would try to refuse it, but she insisted. "I will throw it away if you don't eat it," she'd threaten. Tears would fill my eyes, and even though I was very hungry, the rice would form a lump in my throat as I tried to force it down.

I know now that Mama was starving and gave me her rice so that I would not starve with her. Yet even with her food, my face swelled and my belly stuck out, something that often happens to starving children.

Uncle Abdullah would yell at me. "You are a useless child! Look at you. How ugly you are. You have the spots of a leopard. I am wasting food and money on you. I will not even get a bride-price in return. Who would want to marry a girl who looks like a dangerous beast of the jungle?"

Oh, how I hated my uncle then. I wanted to shout back at him, but I didn't dare. Instead I ran to my mother and curled up in her arms.

Chapter 3

WHEN THE RAIN CAME

The dry season seemed to last forever the year that my father died, making food even scarcer. I breathed a sigh of relief when I awoke early one morning and smelled the scent of rain in the air. Clouds were forming on the horizon. *Ah, the wet season will soon be here, and fruit will grow wild on the trees, and the animals in the bush will grow fat,* I told myself.

I couldn't wait to tell Mama, but she was sleeping peacefully, and I didn't want to wake her. She had been sick for several days. The night before she had vomited so much that she had a nosebleed.

Most of the night I had heard Mama tossing and turning. Just before dawn I heard her sigh loudly three times and finally grow quiet. I smiled to myself, relieved that she was asleep. I brought out my father's notebook and pen, and started to write, knowing that when Uncle Abdullah awoke, I would need to hide them again.

Eventually everyone else got up, leaving only Mama and Uncle Abdullah asleep. I started to worry. If Uncle Abdullah awoke and found my mother asleep, she would be beaten again. Worse yet, he wouldn't give her any more food. When I heard my uncle, I leaped from my grass mat and hurried to her.

"Mama! Mama, wake up," I urged as I shook her shoulder. "Uncle Abdullah will beat you if you do not wake up. Please, Mama! Please, Mama!" I begged over and over again as I shook her harder and harder.

Auntie Huda rushed over and saw blood on Mama's face. "How long has Jemi been sick?" she asked Auntie Yeabu.

"Days," Auntie Yeabu responded.

"Fool!" Auntie Huda yelled. "She has Lassa fever." She looked at me strangely and asked her sister wives, "Has the spotted devil child been sick too?"

Auntie Yeabu shook her head no, too frightened to speak.

Auntie Huda banished me to the yard. I ran outside and crouched close to the doorway, listening to them argue about Lassa fever.

Maybe the refugees who piled into the refugee camps close by had carried it. Maybe Auntie Huda was right, and my mother had been asking for trouble when she helped the man with the missing hand.

"Mama!" I called from the doorway. "Please, may I come in?"

Auntie Yeabu slipped away from the other wives and came to me. She picked me up and covered my eyes with her *lapa*, the long, colorful scarf that was wrapped around her and lay across her shoulder. I pushed the *lapa* away, but Auntie Yeabu said, "No, leave it. You don't want to see them carrying off your mother's body to be buried."

Until that moment I had not realized that my mother was dead. Suddenly I was overwhelmed by the thought that she was gone forever. I began to scream. Grief-stricken, I sobbed, "Please! Please! I want to be with my mama! Bury me too! I don't want to be alive! Nobody loves me!"

"Hush!" Auntie Yeabu begged. "I wouldn't put it past Abdullah to toss you into the grave with your mother."

But I couldn't be quiet. I cried and howled while she held me even tighter for fear that I would jump into the hole that Uncle Abdullah and the village men were digging.

Finally I escaped Auntie Yeabu's clutches as they tossed shovelfuls of dirt over my mother's body, but I was too late. I broke my fingernails as I tried to claw my way through the dirt to her, when Uncle Abdullah grabbed me and tossed me toward his wives. "Control this crazy child!" he roared.

After my mother was buried, Uncle Abdullah burned her belongings, afraid that they had been tainted by the fever. Now I had nothing to remember her by.

Uncle Abdullah turned away from my tearstained face. He had only one concern. He asked, "What will I do if Usman catches this disease?" Then he checked all of my cousins for signs of Lassa fever.

"Mabinty brings us nothing but trouble. It is the spots," Uncle Abdullah's first wife mumbled to her sister wives. "That and her reading. Only a devil child can read when so young. She has brought nothing but bad luck to this family. It is time to be rid of her."

I was used to having my mother sleep close to me at night. She would wrap her arms around me and sing me to sleep, her voice carrying me to a place where I could forget my misery. Without her, I tossed and turned until my uncle nudged me with his foot and said, "Get your belongings and follow me."

I had no idea where he was planning to take me, but I knew that I would want my writing notebook and pen wherever I was going. I hid them in a piece of cloth and tied it around my chest, under my dress. I patted myself, satisfied that they were flat enough that my uncle would not notice them. Then I rolled up the grass mat my mother had woven for me and lifted it onto my shoulder.

I followed Uncle Abdullah down the winding road of

orange dirt that ran past our home. "Where are we going?" I asked in a voice hoarse from crying. Uncle Abdullah only grunted in response, so I didn't give him the satisfaction of asking again, but I couldn't stop my tears. I missed my parents, and without them by my side, I feared what the future would bring.

Soon we started seeing more and more people on the road, traveling with their meager belongings on their heads. Uncle Abdullah spoke with them, and I learned that they were walking the 147 kilometers to Makeni in order to escape the debils.

"Won't the debils just follow everyone to Makeni?" I asked, hiccuping from so much crying, but Uncle Abdullah ignored my question. He poked at my legs with his walking stick, prodding me to walk faster.

"Your daughter looks tired. If you wish, she may climb into my cart," a ragged man on the road said. "I will only charge you a small amount . . . only five leones."

Uncle Abdullah snorted. "I will not pay even one leone. She can walk . . . and she isn't my daughter," he answered gruffly, clearly insulted by the man's assumption that he had fathered such an ugly child.

Uncle Abdullah and I followed the flow of people toward Makeni. Suddenly the sky rumbled and the clouds burst. The thunder drowned out my sobs, and the raindrops mixed with my tears.

I held my bundle closer to my chest as I plodded through the mud, which sucked at my rubber sandals.

Finally the mud swallowed my right sandal. I walked with one sandal and one bare foot, but soon the mud claimed my second sandal too.

Most of the walkers took shelter under the trees and brush, but Uncle Abdullah and I walked on and on. Then a truck stopped, and a voice called out. Uncle Abdullah's face lit up when he recognized Pa Mustapha, a friend from the marketplace. The friend beckoned Uncle Abdullah over to the truck and said something to him.

Suddenly Uncle Abdullah picked me up and threw me into the open bed of the truck, where I landed in the several inches of rainwater that sloshed at the bottom. Then he climbed into the dry cab.

The truck bounced down the road toward Makeni, and I bounced with it as I wrapped myself in my grass mat and continued to cry for the loss of all my happiness. Eventually I fell sound asleep, hungry, wet, and sadder than I had ever felt before.

•→• *Chapter 4* •→•

AT THE ORPHANAGE

The rain had stopped and the last rays of the sun were disappearing when I awoke. Uncle Abdullah opened the tailgate of the truck and crooked his finger to beckon me out. Then he tipped his nose in the direction of a gate without saying a word to me. I stared at a large sign, but it wasn't in Arabic, so I couldn't read it.

I hopped out and followed him without argument. "My mat! I forgot my mat. Wait!" I shouted to Pa Mustapha, but he was gunning the motor and didn't hear me. He pulled away before I could hop back up and get my grass mat.

Uncle Abdullah gave me a shove toward the gate, not caring that I had lost my only remaining connection to my mother. Out of nowhere, a girl appeared from behind the gate. She crouched down and stared at us. "Don't just sit there staring," Uncle Abdullah grumbled at her. "Go and find the director," he ordered.

The girl leaped to her feet, ran to a nearby building, and called out, "Papa Andrew! A man and a pikin are here to see you."

A man in tan pants, a blue shirt, and brown shoes with laces came out of the building. "Welcome to the Safe Haven Orphanage," he said. Then he introduced himself to Uncle Abdullah as Andrew Jah, the director of the orphanage.

My head jerked up, and I stared at the man. Had I heard him correctly? Had he said *orphanage*? Was I now nothing more than an orphan? I had no one to love me or protect me . . . no one to think that I was special. These thoughts tumbled through my mind as I heard my uncle explain, "My brother has been killed. His wife recently died. I bring you my young niece, their daughter. I am her guardian, but I cannot care for her. I have three wives and many children of my own, so I cannot waste food on her. Besides, she is an ugly, sharp-tongued, evil-tempered child with spots. I will never get a bride-price for her. I am sure you understand."

Andrew Jah crouched before me and asked, "What is your name?"

"Mabinty Bangura," I promptly answered.

"What language do you speak?" the director asked in Krio.

When I hesitated, Uncle Abdullah swatted my head. Andrew Jah began to ask the same question in Mende, but I interrupted him in Krio, saying, "I speak Krio, Mende, Temne, Limba, and Arabic."

"So many languages for such a small pikin!" Andrew Jah exclaimed.

"I learned them in the market when I helped my parents in their stall."

At that very moment, my papa's pen fell from under my dress and landed at the director's feet. When I tried to retrieve it, the tie around my chest loosened and the notebook slipped out too. "What is this you were carrying under your dress?" Andrew Jah asked, pointing his nose toward my bundle.

I carefully unwrapped the cloth from around the notebook, relieved to discover that it was not too wet, and held it out to the director with shaking hands. He took the notebook from me and carefully turned the pages. "What have we here?" he asked with surprise.

"It is my notebook," I answered quietly, afraid he would take it away.

"And who did all of this?" He pointed to the writing.

"I did."

"Do you mean to tell me that you are only a small pikin, yet you can read and write Arabic?" the director asked, startled.

I nodded, and he looked at my uncle and said, "This child shows great promise. Our orphanage is full, but I will make room for her under one condition. You cannot return to claim her."

"I have no intention of doing that," Uncle Abdullah said. "I am glad enough to be rid of her."

Then the director invited us into a small room where he gave my uncle some papers to sign. The papers were in English, which my uncle could not read, so the man read them to him and translated them into Krio as I waited quietly and listened carefully. Many of the words were too complicated for me to understand, but I did get the gist of the papers' content. They said that I would be educated and sent to live with a family in another country.

"What other country?" Uncle Abdullah asked.

"The United States of America," Andrew Jah answered, and then he showed my uncle where to sign his name. My heart beat loudly at the words *United States of America*. The name of that country had been special to my parents. They had often spoken of someday taking me there. "It is a place where education is free—even for girls!" my papa had said.

When the director saw that Uncle Abdullah did not know how to sign his name, he removed a small black pad from his drawer, rolled my uncle's thumb on the pad, and pressed it onto the paper, leaving a neat thumbprint on the document. "Now I can prove that you were in agreement with me," Andrew Jah said.

"How much will you be paying me for the child?" Uncle Abdullah asked.

"We do not pay for children. The fact that we will feed them, care for them, educate them, and find them good homes is payment enough to most parents," the director said.

"I am not her parent. My own children are not spotted, like her," Uncle Abdullah retorted. He snatched the thumbprinted paper away. "I could just as easily sell her to a cocoa plantation," he shouted as he seized my arm and began dragging me through the door.

I grabbed the door frame and held on tightly. I wanted to go to the United States of America, but my uncle was big and strong, so he pried me away with little difficulty. I bit him, clinging to his leg with my teeth like a rabid dog.

"Wait!" Andrew Jah cried out, interceding. He coaxed my teeth off my uncle. Then he said the words that Uncle Abdullah so obviously longed to hear: "I have some money for you. We do not ordinarily pay for children, but we sometimes help their families when they are in need." He unlocked a metal drawer in a cabinet and removed some paper money. He held it out to my uncle.

"Ah yes. This will help me feed my hungry family," Uncle Abdullah said as he fondled the bills. Then he turned on his heel and left me behind without so much as a goodbye. I wasn't sad to see him go, but I would miss some of my cousins and Auntie Yeabu. I hadn't even been allowed to say goodbye to them.

The director placed his hand on my shoulder and said,

"You will call me Papa Andrew now, because in this place I'll be your papa. Do you understand?"

My stomach did flip-flops. It made me feel sick to call this strange man Papa. Before I could answer him, the director turned me over to a woman he called Auntie Fatmata, a village woman who worked and lived at the orphanage. Her mouth was turned down in a frown. She rolled her eyes at me and grunted. I could tell that she didn't like me.

When Auntie Fatmata saw me hopping from foot to foot, she led me to an outbuilding with toilets, which were really only holes in the ground, covered with a wooden plank. She told me to be careful, because children had occasionally fallen into the holes. "And watch out for the snakes," she warned. Then she laughed and walked out, leaving me alone in the darkness.

When I finished in the outhouse, Auntie Fatmata was waiting outside for me. She walked me to a building near Papa Andrew's office. It contained a large room where many girls slept two by two on grass mats upon the floor. Auntie Fatmata pointed to a mat where one girl sat, as though awaiting my arrival. She was the girl from the gate.

I was about to say, "I have my own mat, woven by my mother," when I remembered that I had left it behind in the truck. I felt a sudden pang in my chest. That mat had been my only link to my mother, and I had lost it. I dropped, like a limp doll, onto the girl's mat, shivering in my wet clothes.

My shoulders shook as I began to sob into my arms.

"Hush, hush," the girl beside me whispered. "If you awaken Auntie Fatmata with your crying tonight, she will beat you with her willow switch."

The thought of a beating caused me to cry harder. The girl began to pat my back and sing softly, just like my mother would do whenever I had a bad dream. The girl's sweet voice slowly lulled me into a surprisingly sound sleep.

·➤· *Chapter 5* ·➤·

NUMBER TWENTY-SEVEN

Bright sunlight streamed through the window and into my eyes, awakening me. "Mama . . . Papa," I whispered, and then I remembered. They were gone. My home was gone. The life I had known was gone. I was sleeping in a room full of strangers in a strange place . . . an orphanage.

I rolled over and looked at the girl beside me. She was frowning. "What's wrong?" I asked, thinking that, in the daylight, she had seen my spots and regretted sharing her mat with me.

She wrung her hands together as though she was afraid to tell me something. Then she whispered, "I am so very sorry. I've wet the mat."

I bolted upright and stared down at the mat. Sure enough, a dark stain spread over it. I bit my tongue, remembering how kind she had been to me the night before. "It will dry," I said as I helped her roll up the grass mat and carry it into the yard, where we spread it out to dry in the morning sun.

"Hurry," the girl urged after we completed our chore. "The aunties will soon be calling our numbers for breakfast."

"What numbers?" I asked.

"You'll hear," she said. Then she grabbed my hand and pulled me along behind her.

Outside, all of the other orphans gathered to wait for breakfast. They were chattering as loudly as the monkeys in a mango tree until I stepped into the sunny yard. Then they stopped and stared. I knew that they were staring at my spots. I looked down at the ground, ashamed.

"Don't look down," my new friend said. "Hold your chin up high." Then she smiled at me and pulled me toward the group.

Two aunties lugged a large cook pot into the yard. One stood over the pot with a ladle in her hand. "That is Auntie Sombo. She isn't evil, just shy and a bit stupid," my friend whispered. "Auntie Fatmata . . . well, she is the evil one," she explained as she gestured toward the tall, thin auntie who called out, "Number One, Kadiatu Mansarey; Number Two, Isatu Bangura; Number Three, Sento Dumbaya . . ." On and on she went as she called up most of the twenty-three girls and three boys who lived at the orphanage.

Just then I realized that I didn't even know my new friend's name, but I was too scared to speak while the auntie spoke. I waited for her to step forward so that I could learn it. "Number Twenty-Six, Mabinty . . ." I started to step forward, but my friend tugged at my dress, and I stopped in my tracks just as Auntie Fatmata called out the family name: "Suma." My new friend stepped forward to accept her bowl of rice. We had the same first name.

Finally the auntie called, "Number Twenty-Seven, Mabinty Bangura." I hurried to claim my food, and I immediately noticed that my bowl was not as full as most of the others had been. I looked at Mabinty Suma's bowl. Her bowl was only a bit fuller than mine, as was the bowl of Number Twenty-Five, Mariama Kargbo. I understood that it was not a good thing to be Number Twenty-Seven, because the rice ran out by the time the aunties got to the last girl.

When I turned with my bowl in my hands, I saw Mabinty Suma wave to me. "Mabinty Bangura, come eat with me," she said. I smiled because I had a friend. I had never had a friend before, just cousins.

I crouched down beside Mabinty Suma, and we began talking. Then she scooped up some of the rice with the fingers of her left hand and shoveled it into her mouth. I gasped. Everyone, even the youngest children, knew that you should eat with your right hand and use the toilet with your left hand.

Mabinty Suma looked up at me. Before I could even utter a word, she said, "I am Number Twenty-Six because I am left-handed . . . and because I wet my mat." She added in a whisper, "The aunties hate me more for my left-handedness than my bed-wetting. Other girls wet their beds because they are just as afraid as I am of wandering off to the toilet in the dead of night."

Suddenly I realized that, as Number Twenty-Seven, *I* was the least favored child in the entire orphanage. No wonder I had received the smallest serving of rice! I felt the heat rise to my face. My spots were on fire. I thought that they were glowing so brightly that everyone would look at them.

Just then Auntie Fatmata noticed our mat. "Look, Sombo, can you believe that Number Twenty-Six has peed on her mat yet again? Is she too lazy or too stupid to get up in the night and go to the toilets?"

Auntie Sombo grinned and bobbed her head in agreement. Some of the children grinned along with her, while others looked at their feet. I could tell just by looking at their faces which ones had left wet mats in the sleeping room. Surely Auntie Fatmata was smart enough to know that Mabinty Suma was not the only bed wetter.

Auntie Fatmata grabbed her switch, and Mabinty Suma's eyes welled up with tears. "Come here, Number Twenty-Six," the auntie ordered.

Before thinking, I stepped forward and stood between

Auntie Fatmata and Mabinty Suma. "No, don't hit her. That is unfair. You know that she's not the only one to wet her sleeping mat."

The auntie threw her head back and cackled. "Listen to the ugly one, Sombo. This spotted child, the ugliest girl I have ever seen, thinks that she can tell me what to do." Auntie Fatmata raised her switch and struck me first and then Mabinty Suma. She struck us over and over again, raising welts all over our bodies. Finally she said to me, "Now you are striped as well as spotted."

Mabinty Suma was crying loudly, but I was too angry to cry. My anger burned inside me like a fire. Papa had once read me a story about fire-breathing dragons. I wished that I were a dragon and could shoot out my anger in a breath of fire.

Later, while the other children played soccer, the aunties punished us by putting us to work feeding and bathing the babies. I liked babies, so I didn't mind this job at all. They were funny and sweet and didn't care that I had spots.

When the babies were clean and their bellies were full, we went back to the sleeping room with our grass mat. Just in time too, because the sky split open and the rain fell.

Once inside, twenty-seven pairs of hands played hand-clapping games. The sound bounced against the walls and ricocheted across the room from end to end. Hand clapping led to singing, and singing to dancing.

I tried to join in, but whenever I approached a group,

the girls would turn their backs to me. Some chirped through their teeth to show disdain or disgust. Others ran away, shouting, "Devil child! Leopard girl! I don't want to catch your spots."

Only Mabinty Suma would play with me. We were the outcasts, but I was going to change that, so I walked to the center of the room. My father had always said I had an active imagination, and I was good at inventing stories and games. So I decided to win friends for Mabinty Suma and myself.

"I have a new indoor game," I announced. All eyes turned to me, because in a world without any playthings other than a ragged ball, a new game is always welcome. "This is a game that everyone must play. And I mean *everyone*," I added, "or it will not be much fun." When I didn't hear hissing, I continued. "To play the game, we must sit in a circle."

I actually didn't have a game in mind in the first place and had to make one up on the fly. "In this game we will tell the scariest story anyone has ever heard. One girl will start the story, and each girl after her will add to the story. The last girl in the circle will end the story."

"What about the boys?" Omar, the tallest and brightest of the three boys, interrupted.

I rolled my eyes at him and chirped, but let them join us in the circle.

"I should be the one to begin this game," bossy Omar announced.

"It is Mabinty Bangura's idea," a girl named Kadiatu said. Omar began to protest, but he was outnumbered. "You should begin," Kadiatu told me, and so I did.

"In the jungle there is a half man, half leopard that eats children."

Everyone screamed, and the next girl added a line to the story while we all shivered and giggled. By the end of the game I had made twenty-five more friends.

···· Chapter 6 *····*

A VICTORY

"Do you have another game for us?" Sento Dumbaya asked the following day as the rain drummed on the tin roof.

"Yes, I do," I lied. Within minutes I invented another game, which involved singing and dancing as well as storytelling.

Every day of that rainy season, my heart leaped when someone asked, "Do you have another game for us?" I could deal with the mean aunties and the small amount of rice if I had friends.

I refused to show that I was afraid of Auntie Fatmata, even though I really was, just like everyone else. When Auntie Fatmata raised her hand to strike my face,

I didn't wince. When her switch whistled through the air and struck me, leaving welts, I didn't cry. The aunties loved to tug on our tightly braided cornrows, because it hurt so much but left no evidence of their abuse. This was important to them. Andrew Jah needed to send our pictures to America, so he did not want to see bruises on us.

When the aunties tugged on my cornrows, I squeezed my eyes closed. The pain took my breath away, but I wouldn't cry until I was out of sight of both aunties.

The more stoic I appeared, the more Auntie Fatmata tried to make me cry.

One night, when Mabinty Suma and I were sound asleep, Auntie Fatmata ground chili peppers into a fine powder. Then, just before morning, she sprinkled it all over my face until it filled my nostrils, eyes, and mouth.

I sat up and began to scream. My face felt like it was on fire. My eyes streamed with fiery tears.

I could hear Auntie Fatmata cackling. The louder I screamed, the happier she sounded. She had finally succeeded in making me cry. As Mabinty Suma dragged me, stumbling, to the wash bucket, I swore that I would get my revenge.

"We should tell Papa Andrew," Mabinty Suma suggested. I smiled at my best friend. Despite our nearly identical names, we were very different. She turned to adults to solve her problems. I did not.

"If I tell Papa Andrew, he will yell at Auntie Fatmata. That will make it even worse. I have to fix this on my own."

"But how?" she asked.

"I will find a way."

While I was trying to find a way to get even with Auntie Fatmata, the mosquitoes hatched and most of us got malaria. Auntie Fatmata didn't torture us so much while we were sick with fever, vomiting, and diarrhea. But one night soon after I began to get better, Auntie Fatmata made one of the younger children go to the bathroom on my hair and face while I was asleep. I woke up gagging.

Mabinty Suma grabbed my hand and led me outside. I sobbed while she tried her best to clean our grass mat and me. Then it started to rain.

"Come in! Come in now!" Auntie Fatmata screamed, her voice drowned out by thunder as I stood outside, hoping that the lightning wouldn't strike me. I wondered if I might be better off if it did.

Suddenly a lightning bolt struck the ground beside us. Mabinty Suma jumped like a startled cat, but I stayed still. "We could have been killed!" she shrieked.

"A lightning bolt won't kill me," I bragged.

"And why not? Do you have voodoo powers?"

That was it! Mabinty Suma had given me the idea that I needed to fight off Auntie Fatmata. "Yes," I answered.

"I am a witch. Come, I'll show you!" I shouted into the rain as I grabbed her arm and dragged her inside.

I had always been very flexible, and my skin stretched like soft rubber. I used to scare my cousins by flipping my eyelids inside out. Now I decided to put my "talent" to work.

Auntie Fatmata stood inside with her flicking switch. I turned my eyelids inside out and rolled my eyeballs upward. I held my hands out in front of me and said in a deep voice, "I am a witch. I will place a spell on you if you harm me." The aunties were superstitious, and we lived in a place where many people practiced voodoo, so I knew my trick would scare them.

With my eyes rolled into my head, I couldn't see the aunties, but later Mabinty Suma and the other girls told me that their eyes had bugged out and their mouths had hung open with shock. I didn't need to see them to know that I had frightened them badly, because they never again dared to lay a hand on me.

⤞ *Chapter 7* *⤝*

THE GIFT OF THE HARMATTAN

When the rainy season ended, we started school at the orphanage. Because I could read Arabic, I was placed in a class with older children. Together we began learning English and mathematics from Teacher Sarah. She lived nearby in Makeni and visited us every day. She was smart, kind, and gentle, and she reminded me of my mother, so I worked hard to make her proud of me.

One day, after hearing Auntie Fatmata ridicule me for my spots, Teacher Sarah took me aside and said, "Only the ignorant and superstitious will care about your spots. Papa Andrew is trying to send all of you to the United States of America. There you will be placed with a mama and papa who will not give a hoot about your spots. They will care only about your head."

I reached a hand to my tight, thin braids. They had turned orange with malnutrition, and my hair was falling out. I must have looked doubtful about her words, because Teacher Sarah smiled and said to me, "I mean that they will care about what is inside of your head . . . your intelligence . . . your ability to learn."

After Teacher Sarah told me that, I worked even harder than before. I wanted to please my unknown American parents and my beloved teacher. And on the day that a red truck arrived at the orphanage gate, I got my chance.

Usually the dry season brought the rice harvest, but this year, because of the debils, we were without food. When the driver of the truck began unloading huge white bags at the gate, I sounded out the letters until I could read the red-and-blue print. "Mealie meal: super maize meal. Food!"

The aunties set about boiling the mealie meal in the rice pot. It didn't taste as good as rice or cassava, but it was healthier and filled our bellies.

"Who sent us this food?" I later asked Papa Andrew.

"Americans, the ones who are coming in March," he answered.

Americans were coming in March! I had never seen an American. Nor had any of the other girls. We were so excited about the visit that we couldn't sleep that night.

"The Americans will be white," Kadiatu announced from her mat across the room.

"White!" most of the girls exclaimed at once.

"What does a white person look like?" a girl named Yeabu asked.

"I've heard that they are the color of our mealie meal, and you can see the sky through their eyes," Kadiatu answered.

"Are they ghosts?" Mabinty Suma asked.

"No, they are human, like us, and they are all doctors or nurses. I know because my brother met some Americans," Kadiatu informed us.

"Where?" I asked.

"At the hospital, when he had an operation on his face. My brother told me that the doctors wore green robes and masks over their faces," she continued.

With my belly now full for the first time in a long time, I could think about something other than sickness and hunger. As I lay there in the dark, I thought about life in America, but despite Teacher Sarah's optimism, I worried that no American mother and father would want a spotted child.

I fell asleep, desperately missing my mama and papa. It was my birthday the next day, and I longed for them more than ever.

• ◆ •

When I awoke the next morning, the air was thick with orange dust. I could not even see the sun, and the force of the Harmattan wind almost knocked me over. Auntie Fatmata told us to stay inside, but I was sure that I heard my father's voice carried by the wind. "Come with me, Mabinty Suma," I said to my friend. "I want to walk to the gate to see if my father has come calling for me."

"You are crazy, Mabinty Bangura. Your parents are dead, so how can your papa be at the gate?"

"But I never saw my papa's dead body, and I hear his voice," I insisted.

"That is just the wind calling," Mabinty Suma scoffed.

I shook my head. "Maybe he didn't die. Maybe he is alive, and he has come to visit me for my birthday," I declared as I tugged at her arm.

Mabinty Suma rolled her eyes and whined, "If we go, Auntie Fatmata will be angry."

"She won't beat me. She's afraid of me," I reminded her.

"Ha! Well, she isn't afraid of me. *You* are the witch child, not me, Mabinty Bangura."

What my friend said was true, so I patted her shoulder and said, "You can stay here. I'm not afraid to go alone." Then I pulled my T-shirt up over my nose and forced my way against the headwind. The particles of sand stung my skin like needles as I raced toward the gate.

I had run far when I heard Mabinty Suma coughing and calling my name. She was nearly invisible in the swirling clouds of dust. I retraced my steps to her, and hand in hand we headed for the gate.

We did not find my papa when we reached the gate. My heart sank as I watched long lines of strangers hurrying by. Men were pushing wheelbarrows filled with all their worldly goods. Women and girls with baskets of their belongings trailed behind them, babies in *lapa*s clinging to their backs.

"Where are you going?" I called out to a girl about my age.

"The war has come to our town. We are running away from the debils. You should run away too," she answered, and kept going.

I looked at Mabinty Suma and asked, "Should we run away?"

"How can we do that?" she asked. "We have no parents to protect us."

I peered through the wrought-iron gate, hoping that someone would come to take me away. Just then I was slapped in the face. "Ugh! Trash!" I exclaimed, but it wasn't trash at all. I had been attacked by the pages of a magazine. The magazine was stuck in the gate, exactly where my face had been. I reached my hand through and grabbed it.

It was filled with shiny pages printed with pictures of white people. I squinted to look at it, though I was nearly blinded by the dust.

I grabbed Mabinty Suma, and together we ran to the shelter of a tree. "Look! This is what white people look like," I said as I held the fluttering magazine out to her.

"Why are they dressed so funny?" she asked, giggling as she held it inches away from her eyes.

I looked at the cover. A white lady was wearing a very short, glittering pink skirt that stuck out all around her. She also wore pink shoes that looked like the silk fabric I had once seen in the marketplace, and she was standing on the very tips of her toes. "Isn't that a funny way to walk?" Mabinty Suma asked.

"Hmm, I think that she might be dancing," I said.

"Dancing! On tippy-toe? It's impossible to do that!" my friend exclaimed.

"Oh no. I think that I could do it, if I tried hard enough," I said. Then I leaped to my feet and stood on the tips of my naked toes. I dropped back to the soles of my feet, and I twirled around, full of joy, despite the wind that stung my face and blew into my open mouth.

"Someday I will dance on my toes like this lady. I will be happy too!" I shouted into the wind.

At that moment we heard Auntie Fatmata screaming for us to come back. "Hurry! Go. I'll follow you," I said. Then I quickly ripped the cover off of the magazine as the wind tried to tear it from my hands, and folded it in half, and in half again. I stuffed it into my underwear, the one item of clothing that I owned. I ran back to the building with the magazine flapping in my hand.

When I saw how angry Auntie Fatmata was, I said, "Look, Auntie Fatmata, I have a gift for you. It's a white person's magazine and it has many wonderful pictures."

Ah, the look of confusion on her face was priceless. It must have been very difficult to allow the words *Thank you, Number Twenty-Seven* to spill from her lips.

Later I heard Auntie Fatmata complaining loudly to Auntie Sombo. "Number Twenty-Six and Number Twenty-Seven were down by the gate in all of this wind. Stupid girls. Don't they know that nothing good ever comes of the Harmattan?"

I grinned behind my hands. Then I stood on my toes and tried to twirl around the room, nearly tripping over the legs of the other girls. "Ow! Oof! What are you doing, Mabinty Bangura? You are stepping on us," Yeabu complained.

"I'm celebrating the Harmattan!" I exclaimed, giddy with excitement, knowing that some good does come from the Harmattan.

Chapter 8

WHITE LADIES AND FAMILY BOOKS

The following day, when we had finished our lessons with Teacher Sarah, I lagged behind, as usual. "Do you have to leave now?" I asked her, as I did every afternoon, while she gathered her belongings for the long walk home.

"Mabinty Bangura, what is on your mind?" Teacher Sarah asked.

"I found a treasure," I answered as I carefully unfolded the picture I had kept hidden since the night before. "I'm trying to read these words, but most are too difficult," I said, and I held out the creased cover.

"Oh, this is a picture of a ballerina," she said, pointing to a word. "This word, *ballerina*, is an Italian word. It means 'little dancer.' The woman in this picture is a ballet dancer."

"What is ballet?" I asked.

"It is a kind of dance. It takes many years of practice to become good at it," she explained as we walked toward the gate.

"Do you think that I could learn it?" I asked.

"Maybe . . . if you take ballet lessons," Teacher Sarah answered.

"Could you give me ballet lessons?"

"Oh, I only wish that I had so much grace and talent," she said. "No, I cannot teach ballet, but I have a book about ballet at my parents' home in Freetown. The next time I visit, I'll bring it back for you," she said, with a loving smile on her face.

I was so excited about the book that I ran hooting and hollering across the orphanage yard. Papa Andrew frowned at me.

"You are late, as usual. I am telling the other orphan pikins about the American ladies who will soon be visiting. Now sit down and be quiet."

I hurriedly flopped into the space beside Mabinty Suma and listened as Papa Andrew warned us to be on our best behavior. He frowned at me again when I raised my hand and asked, "Are they bringing us back to America with them?"

"If you hadn't been late, Mabinty Bangura, you would

have known the answer to that question. No, not now. They are coming to photograph you and examine each of you. They'll also immunize you," he said.

I nodded knowingly. I knew what a photograph was, and I had been examined by a doctor once, an African doctor, but I didn't know what the word *immunize* meant. I raised my hand to ask Papa Andrew, but he ignored me. He had told me many times before that I asked too many questions for my own good. I decided to just wait and find out for myself what that long word meant.

The following morning we got up early to bathe and have our hair freshly braided. Papa Andrew lined us up at the gate by height, with the smallest first and the tallest last. He made us sing one of the English songs that Teacher Sarah had taught us as a car drove through the orphanage gate. We sang my favorite, "*Lapa, Lapa, Lapa* on My Shoulder," and, eager to please, I sang at the top of my lungs.

My voice faltered when three ladies climbed out of the car. They were the strangest-looking women I had ever seen. They didn't look at all like the lovely ballerina in my magazine. These women had bright red faces and wild, frizzled hair. One had yellow hair, the second had orange hair, and the third had brown hair. They all had different-colored eyes too.

"Ah yes. They are nurses, for sure. I can tell," Kadiatu murmured with a voice of authority.

"I didn't know that white people came in different colors, like Teacher Sarah's crayons," I whispered into Mabinty Suma's ear.

The tallest woman said to us, "I loved your singing! What language was it?" When Papa Andrew translated her compliment into Krio for us, we all giggled because we thought that we had sung in English.

Papa Andrew snapped his fingers and pointed at us one by one. We leaped to attention and helped the ladies carry boxes from their car to our classroom. When the boxes were unpacked, the ladies lined us up outside the classroom. The other girls hung back, but I pushed to the head of the line, tugging a nervous Mabinty Suma behind me.

One of the women smiled at me as she wrote my name on the first page of her notebook. Next, the second lady measured my height and the thickness of my arm. Then she weighed me. When she looked at the numbers on the scale, she pursed her lips and frowned. I began to worry. Maybe I didn't weigh enough to go to America.

The third lady squirted sweet juice into my mouth. It tasted pretty good, and I decided that if this was my immunization, I wouldn't mind more.

Suddenly the second lady wrapped her arms tightly around me. I began to scream as the third lady grabbed my arm and was about to stab it with a needle. I wiggled and squirmed. I even tried to bite the woman who was holding me, but she didn't let me go.

The stab of the needle didn't last long, and I was

rewarded with something called a lollipop. It was round and orange, and it tasted even better than the sweet juice. Finally the third lady hugged me, patted me, and sent me out the door.

Once free, I strutted up and down the line of girls waiting for their turns. "It's worth getting stabbed by a needle to get this round, sweet thing," I explained as I held up the lollipop.

Mabinty Suma soon came out of the classroom, sucking on a purple lollipop. I gave her a lick of mine, and she let me taste hers. The white American ladies gave us many more lollipops while they were there. They also painted our fingernails. During their visit, Papa Andrew fed us all kinds of treats, like chicken and okra. I was sorry to see the Americans leave, and I wished on a star that they wouldn't forget us.

My wish came true. The American ladies didn't forget us. They sent us brushes for our teeth, barrels of clothes, shoes, screens for our windows, beds, long pipes that carried water from the well to the inside of our compound, and little packets of colored powder called Kool-Aid.

Papa Andrew added the colored powder to our water when it tasted rancid. The Kool-Aid smelled like the lollipops, but it was bitter. It would be a long time before I told this story to someone in America and learned the reason why: the Kool-Aid was supposed to be mixed with sugar, and sugar was expensive.

The best things that the Americans sent us were family books. Papa Andrew explained, "These are books prepared by your new parents, and will be filled with pictures and messages from your new mamas and papas. Each of you will get your own book, except for sisters. They will share, because they will be going to the same family."

From the day Papa Andrew mentioned the books until the day they arrived, we did nothing but imagine what our new American families would look like. I told everyone that my new mother would be young, tall, and slim. She would dance on the tips of her toes. My father would be even taller. They would both be very smart and read a lot.

One night, when we were talking about our new families, Mabinty Suma fell silent. "What's wrong? Why are you so quiet?" I asked her.

Then she burst into tears, saying, "We are going to have different mothers and different fathers. We might not even live in the same village."

I gasped. That thought had not occurred to me. I had simply assumed that because we were best friends and our names were so similar, the same family would adopt both of us. Suddenly, getting adopted and moving to America didn't promise to be as much fun as I had thought it would be. Then the truck arrived with the boxes of family books, and things got worse. Mabinty Suma and every other girl in the orphanage got a family book, but I did not. I felt a big, empty space in my belly. It hurt worse than when I was hungry.

While all of the girls sat in a circle, laughing and sharing the pictures of their new families, I crept off and wandered to the classroom. Teacher Sarah was still there, cleaning. When she heard me enter the classroom, she looked up with surprise and said, "Mabinty Bangura, why aren't you outside, sharing your family book?"

"I didn't get one," I whispered. "Nobody wanted me. I must be too ugly." I burst into tears and ran to Teacher Sarah, who opened her arms wide and rocked me back and forth. "Please," I begged her. "Adopt me. I won't eat too much, and I will help you take care of your new baby," I said as I patted her growing belly. Teacher Sarah stayed with me for a long time that day, trying to comfort me.

·➤· *Chapter 9* ·➤·

THE DEBILS!

The debils had been wandering in and out of our town ever since the Harmattan. They bothered many of the people in town, but they left our orphanage alone. I had heard Papa Andrew tell the aunties and our night watchman that it was safe enough here during the day, but that they should not go into the streets after dark, when the debils were drunk and crazy from drugs.

It was darker than usual when I walked Teacher Sarah to the gate that night. We heard the distant sounds of drunken laughter. "Is it safe to walk home now?" I asked her.

"Yes, if I hurry," she assured me.

I stood at the gate as I did most evenings when Teacher Sarah left. Tonight she moved faster than usual as she headed down the road toward her home. Suddenly, out of the darkness, two debil trucks drove by, lighting up the dirt road and catching Teacher Sarah in their headlights. They stopped, and laughing men and boys leaped to the ground.

"NO-O-O!" I shouted as they surrounded Teacher Sarah. I squeezed my skinny body through the wrought-iron bars of the gate and raced down the road toward her.

When I got there, several debils were holding her down by her wrists and ankles. A big debil who was clearly the leader stood there, shouting, "Boy? Girl?" A large group of debils surrounded him, holding up fistfuls of paper money. The leader then raised his long, curved knife above his head.

When I saw what the debil was about to do, I threw myself on Teacher Sarah.

The debil leader laughed at me, picked me up by my shirt, and flung me aside as though I were no heavier than a bug. Then he slashed downward with his knife and cut into Teacher Sarah. Blood spurted everywhere, covering me from head to toe.

The debil reached inside of Teacher Sarah and pulled out her unborn baby. He examined it and shouted, "A girl!" Several men groaned. They had bet that the baby was a boy, so they had lost their money. Others, who had gambled on a girl, shouted in triumph.

The debil leader laughed just as Teacher Sarah's under-size baby girl drew her first breath and opened her eyes. He then tossed the infant into the bush on the side of the road. I ran into the bush to try to save the baby. If I couldn't save my teacher, at least I might rescue her child, but a young debil dragged me out kicking and screaming. He wasn't much older than me.

The debil leader then turned his attention to me. "What do we have here? Are you causing trouble *again*?" He nodded to the child soldier. The little boy lunged for my chest with his knife, but when he looked into my eyes, he hesitated just long enough for me to take one step backward. The knife only grazed me.

"Kill her, or I will kill you!" the debil leader screamed at the boy.

"Stop, please! Do not kill her, please. She is just a poor orphan pikin. What does it matter to you whether she is dead or alive?" a frantic voice begged. It was Uncle Sulaiman, the night watchman at the orphanage, who must have followed me out. I gasped when I saw him. Didn't he know that the debils wouldn't hesitate to cut off his limbs? However, the debil leader appeared to be amused by Uncle Sulaiman and asked, "Why should I care?"

"You don't . . . you shouldn't. That's why it is just as easy for you to let her go," Uncle Sulaiman said.

The debil leader nodded, as though considering his logic. "Fine, take her. Just keep her out of my way," he ordered.

Sulaiman tossed me over his shoulder and raced back to the orphanage. He brought me to the director, who beat me with a switch for leaving the orphanage.

In a strange way I was almost grateful for the beating, because the sting of the welts took my mind away from the horror that I had witnessed. Papa, Mama, and now Teacher Sarah . . . how could I go on? Then I saw the tearful face of Mabinty Suma.

"Mabinty Bangura! Where were you? I was so worried. I thought you were dead!" she cried. I hugged her tightly, but I couldn't tell her what I had seen. That night I lay trembling, thinking of Teacher Sarah and unable to sleep.

The next morning Papa Andrew announced to us that Teacher Sarah would not be returning to teach us. The other children thought that it was the birth of her baby that kept her away. It would be many months before I could tell anyone what had happened.

The debils' attacks were getting worse and worse, and we began to feel unsafe, even behind our gate. A few days after Teacher Sarah was murdered, we all woke up to what sounded like a bomb exploding in the yard. All of us leaped to the window to see what had happened. "Debils! Hide!" I shouted when my eyes fell upon the camouflaged men who jumped from the green truck that had crashed onto our property.

"Hide? Where?" Kadiatu cried as she gazed about the room, eyes bugged out with panic.

"Under our new beds," Mabinty Suma ordered.

We stayed under our beds for what seemed like forever, though it probably was only a few minutes, before a booted foot kicked open the door. "Tell your orphan pikins to come out," a gruff voice ordered. "I will not harm them."

Then we heard Papa Andrew's voice assure us. "Come out, pikins. You are safe."

One by one we came out from our hiding places. "Hurry!" the debil leader barked as we scrambled to our feet. The sight that greeted us was horrifying. A tall man with grizzled hair was holding a gun to Papa Andrew's head. He was the same man who had attacked Teacher Sarah.

I gripped Mabinty Suma's ice-cold hand. If I were about to be killed, I wanted to die with someone I loved. I could see in the flickering light that several other children did the same. Sisters clung to sisters, friends to friends, as we awaited our fate.

Much to my surprise, the debils did not shoot us or chop off our limbs. Instead the leader ordered Papa Andrew to line us up and lead us out into the darkness of night.

"I hereby declare that this orphanage is now the headquarters of the Revolutionary United Front in Makeni. I will spare your life, the lives of your staff, and the lives of your orphan pikins," the debil leader said to Papa Andrew.

"Where will we live?" Papa Andrew asked.

"In the bush, where we members of the RUF usually make our beds," the leader answered.

"May I get the children's adoption papers and passports from my office?" Papa Andrew asked.

Surprisingly, the debil leader nodded and ordered his second-in-command to escort Papa Andrew to the office.

Mabinty Suma whispered in my ear, "Mabinty Bangura, would you ask the debil man if we can get our family books?"

Without even thinking, I asked, "May we get the books from our American families?"

The debil leader narrowed his eyes. Then he threw his head back and laughed. "Pikin, you are once again trying my patience." But once Papa Andrew returned, the debil leader sent him off to get our family books.

As we got ready to leave, the debil leader warned, "Do not think of escaping to the Guinea border. You will be killed for trying to leave Sierra Leone. Our country needs its people."

I wondered why the debils were killing so many people if this was true, but it was better not to ask.

Papa Andrew, Auntie Fatmata, Auntie Sombo, and Uncle Sulaiman herded us off the orphanage grounds. We left without anything except the family books and the papers that would enable most of us to go to America. We made our way through the jungle and over the mountains to the Guinea border. Yes, that's right. We were heading to the neighboring country of Guinea, despite the threats of the debil leader.

I didn't have a family book to keep me going as we walked through the bush, so I pulled out the folded picture from the magazine. That picture was my only hope. It was my promise of a better life somewhere away from all this madness.

·•· *Chapter 10* ·•·

STEPPING-STONES TO AMERICA

We saw hundreds of dead bodies on our way out of Sierra Leone. The debils had taken machetes to many of the people, but the majority of them, even small children, had been shot in the head. They lay sprawled on the ground with their eyes and mouths open in terror. I could tell how long they had been dead by the stink and by the bugs that crawled over them.

At night we tossed and turned, hungry, afraid, and driven nearly crazy with itching, because most of us had gotten chicken pox. Mabinty Suma tried to comfort us all by singing songs from our days in the orphanage. My favorite was "Let There Be Light," a song that she had made up. That song and the ballerina photo were the two things that reminded me that I was still alive.

One afternoon, when I felt that I could no longer put one foot in front of the other, a voice boomed out of the dense bush. A man in uniform came out, startling us all. We made a beeline for the trees. Papa Andrew nearly dropped the child he was carrying in his effort to stop us. "We are here! We are here! We have reached the Guinea border!" he shouted.

To my eyes one camouflage uniform looked like another. The soldier at the border looked no different from the debils who had terrorized us, but we eventually came out from behind the trees. As we stepped into Guinea, a familiar face emerged from the crowd to greet us. It was Uncle Ali, the Sierra Leone agent of the American adoption agency. He was a mean man, and I wasn't usually pleased to see him, but my heart was happy to see him this time. I knew that he would get my fellow pikins from the border to their new homes in America. But where would I end up? The thought of being left behind made me feel as if I had been stabbed.

Papa Andrew and Uncle Ali piled us into a truck. We were taken to a makeshift village where the huts were made out of thin plastic, making it look like a sprawling garbage-bag town. We were assigned to one of the huts, and we stood staring at each other in the heat as the sun poured down on our shelter. I was so hot, tired, hungry, and sick that I was unsure of whether to cry in self-pity or laugh in celebration of our arrival.

The United Nations refugee camp in Guinea was not a place where we could laugh and play. The local trees, which had once stood tall, had been cut down to be the lodge poles upon which our plastic-bag huts were built. Tree stumps poked out of the ground, making it too dangerous for us to run around.

Before nightfall a worker at the camp warned Papa Andrew that RUF rebels would try to sneak into the camp after dark. "Keep the children inside," he said. "Any unaccompanied child is likely to be kidnapped or killed."

We sat huddled together on the ground inside the hut on that first night. In the morning Papa Andrew left us with Uncle Sulaiman and the aunties while he walked to the nearby town. Later that day, when the sun was at its highest and the inside of the plastic house was hot enough to bake us like cassava, he returned to collect us. "I have made arrangements for us to move into a house in Conakry," he said. "You will be safer there. It is too far away from the border for the RUF to kidnap children."

I had only known the Kenema District of Sierra Leone, where I was born, and the city of Makeni in the Bombali District. Conakry, Guinea, might have been halfway across the world, as far as I knew. "Is Conakry close to America?" I asked.

"No, it is a stepping-stone on the way to America," Papa

Andrew explained. "The international airport is there. That is where we will board our flight out of Guinea to Ghana, and from there you will travel by plane again to America."

My mouth dropped open, and I must have looked stunned, because Papa Andrew asked, "How did you think you would get to America? Walk?"

"I thought we would ride in the back of a truck," I answered.

Papa Andrew laughed. It seemed that he often laughed when I said something. When I had first met him, I thought that he laughed to make fun of me, so I would get mad. Now I knew that he laughed because he thought that I was funny, and I liked that.

"America is across the ocean," he explained.

"Couldn't we ride in a boat?" I asked.

"That would take forever. What is your objection to flying in an airplane?"

"It might fall out of the sky, or I might feel sick up so high," I answered, and he laughed once more.

"A ship might sink, and you would definitely feel sick on a ship," Papa Andrew said. He was the only person in the plastic hut who seemed to find my words funny. Everyone else was too worried to laugh.

He was still shaking his head from side to side and chuckling to himself as he led us out of our plastic house to the road outside the camp. There, a wrinkled old man was waiting for us with a yellow-and-black taxicab. We had been in a truck before, but none of us had ridden inside a car. We climbed into what we believed was the lap of luxury.

All of us pikins squeezed into the back of the taxicab. We sat on laps several children deep as the four adults in our party climbed into the front with the taxi driver. I couldn't see anything because I was buried somewhere under a pile of children. All I can remember from the ride is how sweaty it was and how much I felt like throwing up.

Our little house in Conakry wasn't much different from our orphanage in Makeni. We had no new beds in the Conakry house like the ones the Americans had sent to us in Makeni, so we made do with grass mats.

We also had no teacher and no books in Conakry. Every day I thought of Teacher Sarah and the wonderful storybooks that she had read to us, so my memories of her were both happy and sad.

Papa Andrew and Uncle Ali tried to buy books with the money sent to them by the American adoption agency so that we could continue our lessons, but there were no books to be had . . . at least no books written in English, because French is the official language of Guinea. So the pikins read the family books over and over again.

Of course, I had no family book to read, so I sat alone with a stick, writing words in the dirt.

"What are you doing?" Mabinty Suma asked.

"I am pretending that I have an American family and this is my family book."

"You don't have to pretend, Mabinty Bangura. I'll share my family book with you."

"But that's your family, not mine," I answered, with tears filling my eyes.

"Well, maybe when I meet my new mama, I can ask her if she wants two daughters," Mabinty Suma said.

That cheered me up, so together Mabinty Suma and I read her family book. Together we recited the words "Hello, I am your American mother. Hello, I am your American father. You have three American brothers. Their names are Adam, Erik, and Teddy. Teddy plays the piano."

Each time we read that, we'd ask each other, "What is a piano? How do you play with it?"

Mabinty Suma and I would screech every time we came to the page that said, "This is our family dog. His name is Alaska." He was an enormous dog with long, sharp teeth and furry white hair. He was bigger than the two of us put together. "Do you think he has rabies?" I'd ask, causing us to shriek louder.

"He looks like he wants to eat us!" Mabinty Suma would say, and again we'd scream.

The page I liked best was the one that said, "This is our house at Thanksgiving. Thanksgiving is a holiday when we give thanks and eat turkey."

"This turkey is the biggest chicken I've ever seen," I'd

comment. "I can't wait to eat it." Somehow I had convinced myself that this was my family as well as Mabinty Suma's. When I'd remember that the turkey didn't belong to my family, because I didn't have a family, I'd feel that stabbing pain in my chest again and I'd start to cry.

Mabinty Suma preferred the page that said, "This is your bedroom." In the picture was a bright red bed with a colorful blanket. We could see dolls on the bed, and in the background dresses were hanging. I couldn't help feeling jealous that she'd soon be wearing those dresses and I would be left behind with nothing but my rags.

Later on she noticed that her bed had a top and a bottom. "Look! My bed has two parts! There is enough room for you! I promise: I will ask my new mother if you can sleep on the top of my bed."

Mabinty Suma and her bed with two parts gave me hope.

One day Papa Andrew called a meeting and announced, "Tomorrow we are leaving for the airport. We are going to Ghana. It is another stepping-stone to America. There you will meet your new parents."

For a moment I forgot that I did not have a family. I joined the other children, hooting with joy, until Auntie Fatmata said to me, "Number Twenty-Seven, what are you cheering for? Nobody wanted a spotted child. Papa Andrew told me that you were offered to twelve families, but all of them refused to have you. You are staying in Africa with me."

The thought of staying behind with Auntie Fatmata filled me with terror. I jumped up and ran out of the room. Later Papa Andrew came looking for me. He explained to me that, at the last minute, a family had been found for me. I too would be adopted.

As excited as I was to have an American family, I had grown used to the idea that Mabinty Suma's family was mine too. I had lost everyone else I loved in the world. How was I going to live without my best friend?

·•· Chapter 11 ·•·

INTO A MOTHER'S ARMS

Early the next morning we boarded the plane to Ghana. I was so nervous that I vomited all over my dress and Uncle Ali. The flight attendant brought wet paper towels and tried to wipe me clean, but even when the dress was clean, it still smelled awful.

After the plane landed, I was the first to see the white parents, but I could not stop to scrutinize them and guess which belonged to me. Uncle Ali was angry with me for misbehaving on the flight from Guinea and for vomiting all over his pants. He hauled me past the crowd of onlookers, tugging my arm and walking so fast that my feet flew off the floor. He dragged me into the toilets and spanked me soundly before bringing me back past everyone a second time.

I was so embarrassed and angry that I couldn't stop scowling when I finally exited the gate with the other pikins. Mabinty Suma pinched my arm and said, "If you wear such a grouchy face, the American families will not like you." I ignored her, because I was suddenly distracted by the feet of the women.

I crouched down to examine their shoes, hoping that my mama would be wearing pink dancing shoes. Many of the parents were wearing sneakers. Sneakers were a luxury in Africa, and I desperately wanted a pair, though not quite as much as I wanted pink dancing shoes. The sneakers I saw were in dull colors like gray, tan, black, or white. I did spy one pair of bright red sneakers that set one woman apart from the others. My gaze traveled from her feet to her face, and I recognized the mama in Mabinty Suma's family book. I grabbed Mabinty Suma's arm and tipped my nose in her new mother's direction.

The woman smiled at us. She came up to us and patted our backs. "I'm your new mama," she said to both of us. "You're going to be sisters."

Could this be true? I thought I understood the word *sisters*, but I couldn't believe my ears. I squeezed Mabinty Suma's hand, and then I got so excited that I even pinched her arm. She must have been as happy as I was, because she didn't get mad and pinch me back.

Finally our new mama took hold of our hands and led us away, and we knew that our dream of staying together was coming true. I thought that we would be taken directly to our new home in America—the one with the lake in the yard, the fierce white dog, the piano, and the big Thanksgiving chicken—but we wouldn't be leaving to go to America for a while. We had entered Ghana without visas, and we spent hours waiting for permission to enter that country.

I looked around at my friends. They sat with their new parents, looking scared and uncertain of what awaited them. I didn't feel scared. I had wanted to be Mabinty Suma's sister so badly that I felt sure I would be fine.

Mabinty Suma clung to our new mama as though she had known her for a lifetime. Suddenly Uncle Ali rose from his seat and ripped them apart. He said to Mama, "You have enough to do with one child. I will hold this one." Then he sat down with Mabinty Suma on his lap.

Mabinty Suma had always hated Uncle Ali, so it didn't surprise me when her chin quivered and the tears pooled in her eyes. Mama walked over to Uncle Ali, said something to him, and lifted Mabinty Suma from his lap. I could only understand two words: "Five sons." Whatever she said that day angered him because his eyes blazed with fury. He wasn't used to women standing up to him. When Mama returned to her seat with Mabinty Suma, I couldn't help but grin. I liked this new mother . . . very much.

Later, when I could speak and understand English well,

I learned that Mama had said to Uncle Ali, "I've raised five sons. I can certainly manage these two children." That is when Mama explained to us that in addition to their sons Adam, Erik, and Teddy, she and Papa had adopted two boys with hemophilia, named Michael and Cubby, who had died of AIDS before we arrived in the United States.

After we finally received our visas, we were taken to be examined by doctors. They were African doctors who were paid by the American embassy to screen immigrants to the United States. The doctors took one look at my skin and spoke among themselves, wondering if my spots might be the result of a terrible disease called congenital syphilis.

My new mother stood up to these men too. "This child does not have congenital syphilis, or syphilis of any kind. She has vitiligo."

The doctors and I stared in wonder at Mama. She didn't look like anyone I'd ever seen, with pale yellow hair and eyes the color of the sky. "How do you know? Are you a doctor?" one of the African doctors asked her.

"Actually, I am a teacher of medical students," she answered. The doctors immediately stopped arguing with her. They stamped a paper, and I was approved for entry into the United States.

With a mother like this, I knew I could do anything, even dance in pink shoes.

I didn't realize that my new mother was scared until I gripped her hand and felt that she was trembling. When we sat in the waiting area, she held me close to her. Before that moment I had remained aloof from her, but now everything had changed. She had defended me, protected me, just as my African mother would have done. She was my mother now, and I leaned back into her arms. It had been a long time since I had felt protected.

Soon it was Mabinty Suma's turn to be examined. With her bright eyes and dark, flawless skin, she easily earned the doctors' stamp of approval, though later we would learn that she had some serious medical problems.

When we returned to the waiting area, Mama wrapped her arms around both of us, and we snuggled in close. We were sisters—part of a family now, with the good fortune to have found just the right mama.

Later that day we went to Mama's hotel. Mabinty Suma and I were thrilled to see that it had a real bed, just like the one that Papa Andrew had used at the orphanage. We leaped onto the bed and bounced up and down in a fit of giggles.

Mama laughed and hauled us off the bed. She carried us, still giggling, into another room, where she flicked a little switch on the wall and, like magic, light flooded the space. Mabinty Suma and I tried flicking the switch too, and the lights went off. We pushed the switch up, and they turned on again. We pushed it down, and the lights turned off.

While we were entertaining ourselves with the light switch, Mama turned a knob in a white tub. Water splashed out of the pipe, which our mother called a faucet. She poured a capful of yellow liquid into the water, and bubbles began to fill the tub. Finally Mama helped us climb in. Our first bubble bath! Mabinty Suma and I were thrilled. "Smell me!" I shouted with glee as I held up my hands. I had never smelled so good before.

When we were bathed, our mama wrapped us in towels, led us into the sleeping room, and presented each of us with clean, sweet-smelling clothes. Mine were pretty purple, and Mabinty Suma's were pink.

I had no sooner gotten dressed than I remembered! Off I dashed to find my beautiful ballerina picture inside my old, dirty clothes on the bathroom floor. Thankfully, it was still there.

Mama began to unpack her luggage, pulling out some little dolls, beads, and bags of clothing. And then she found two pairs of sneakers that sparkled with pink glitter. When we stepped into them, lights flashed from our heels.

Even though I loved the glittery sneakers, I stood at my mother's side, patiently waiting for the one thing that I really wanted, while Mabinty Suma gathered up the beads and dolls and spread them over the bed to play. Mama looked down at me and said something. Though I didn't understand a word of her English, I could tell by the sound of her voice that she was asking me a question.

She unzipped all of the suitcases as though inviting me to search through them. Soon I was digging through piles of clothes and toys, checking all the nooks, crannies, and zippered compartments of Mama's luggage. But Mama had not brought me pink dancing shoes. She crouched down in front of me and asked, "What is it that you so desperately want, dear daughter?"

I tried to remember the English words that Teacher Sarah had taught me, but they wouldn't come to my lips. Instead I babbled on in Krio as I tried to explain about the ballerina and the special pink shoes.

My mother shook her head. Clearly she didn't understand me. Finally I pulled out my magazine picture and handed it to her. While she carefully unfolded it, I twirled around the room and stood on the tips of my naked toes.

My American mama gasped. Then she laughed. "So you want to be a ballerina!" she exclaimed in a happy voice.

Ballerina! That was the word that Teacher Sarah had taught me. "Yes," I shyly answered.

My mama placed her hands on my shoulders. Very slowly she said, "Home in America . . . you will dance."

My heart beat rapidly in my chest. I became breathless with excitement. Mama understood me. She knew I wanted to dance. I was almost delirious with joy, knowing that my dream might someday come true.

Chapter 12

MICHAELA, MIA, AND
THE NUTCRACKER

O n our second day in Ghana, Mama realized that
every time she called, "Mabinty," we both came running. Sharing the same first name hadn't mattered in the
orphanage, where we were called by our numbers. But
Mama didn't intend to call us Number Twenty-Six and
Number Twenty-Seven. Instead she pointed at Mabinty
Suma and said, "Mia Mabinty." She pointed at me and
said, "Michaela Mabinty." Our African first names became
our American middle names. One week later, when we
boarded the plane to America, we were already answering
to our American names.

·◆·

I had a fever and slept for most of the long trip to the United States, while Mia enjoyed looking out the plane's windows at the Sahara Desert, reading magazines, and eating mounds of butter during our layover in Germany.

My fever broke temporarily, and I awoke in time for landing at John F. Kennedy International Airport in New York City. From there we were driven south to our Cherry Hill, New Jersey, home in a shiny black car that was finer than any I had seen before. On the way I was so hungry from not eating while conked out on the airplane that I begged for rice. The driver pulled over, and Mama took us inside a building that she called a rest stop, though no one seemed to be resting there.

I was overwhelmed by the amount of food in the rest stop. There wasn't any rice, but Mama bought us whatever we pointed to: hot dogs, fried chicken, orange juice, and ice cream. Mia and I ate everything!

Eventually we pulled up in front of a beautiful blue house surrounded by tall trees. An older, white-haired man and two dark-haired young men came out to greet us. Mia and I knew from our family book that they were our father and our older brothers Teddy and Erik. I also remembered the page that said, "Adam is your oldest brother. He is married and lives one hundred miles away." So I was not surprised that Adam was not there.

I trusted my new papa immediately, but I was leery of

the younger men. I wanted to ask if they were debils, but I was too afraid. I finally decided that, since they were not carrying knives or rifles and since my new mother hugged them, they probably were not debils.

We had held on tightly to the backpacks Mama had given to us the entire way home, because they were the first things that we had ever owned. Now, whether Teddy and Erik were brothers or not, we wouldn't let them touch our backpacks. We hoisted them onto our backs and followed Mama into the house.

In Africa women stick together, and men generally go about their own business. A girl's mother is always her greatest influence, friend, and adviser. I suppose this is why, from that very first day in my new home, I felt a special bond with my new mother.

That first day, as I wandered through the house that belonged to my new family, I was ecstatic to discover the inground pool, and I begged to swim. Mia was less impressed with the pool than she was with the piano in the living room. We both remembered the picture of Teddy playing the piano. Now, as Mia stood across the living room, staring at the strange object, Teddy sat down on a bench and began playing it.

When he touched the white and black keys on the piano, music wafted out of the instrument, and Mia's face lit with joy. In Africa she and I had thought that this large object was a toy, because Mama had written on the photo, "Teddy, playing the piano." We didn't have any idea that a piano made music. After that first day Mia and I often fought over whose turn it was to play the piano.

Because Mia and I had both arrived in the United States sick, we spent a lot of time in the doctor's office, where we were stuck with needles many times. The antibiotics that the doctor prescribed for me healed the terrible case of tonsillitis I had arrived with. The doctor told my mother that if I had remained in Africa another day or two, the infection would have spread through my body, causing sepsis. I surely would have died.

With the exception of the needles, my new world was a wondrous one. The first time I went to the supermarket, I couldn't believe the amount of food that lined the shelves. At first I was reluctant to touch any of it, but then I saw my mama and papa picking up fruits and piling them into a cart, and I joined in. Mia joined me, and together we grabbed at everything in sight. We began running up and down the aisle, filling our arms and our mouths as our parents chased us.

Suddenly Papa grabbed me and tossed me into the front seat of one of the carts. Mama did the same to Mia. I began to cry with frustration until Mama handed me a red box and popped a tiny, wrinkled brown fruit into my mouth. It was sweet and utterly delicious. It didn't take me long to devour the entire box of raisins.

After Mama and Papa had each filled a cart with food,

they stood in a line and gave a woman their small plastic card. I was amazed that we had been given all of this food for free! I wanted one of those plastic cards for myself. That night in bed Mia and I tried to think of ways to make our own plastic cards.

A few days later Mama took us to another, even more enormous building. She called it a mall. It was like the bazaar in Makeni—only it was indoors, cleaner, and better. This time, instead of food, we bought clothes.

I wanted everything that I saw. I ran over to a purple dress and tried to pull it down off its hanger. When Mama said, "No!" I went crazy. All she had to do was swipe her plastic card, and the dress would be mine. "Why! Why!" I shouted.

Mia started grabbing at dresses too. Mama had to pick us up and carry us, kicking and screaming, out of the store. It took quite a few trips to the mall before Mia and I learned that we couldn't have everything that we wanted.

Life in America was fun, with new adventures every day. In the late summer Papa drove us to the seashore. There he lifted us high as breaking waves threatened to knock us down. He dug a deep hole in the sand and collected seashells with us. As we strolled along the beach, Mama pointed across the water and said, "I first met you there, on the other side of the ocean, in Africa." I looked in fascination. I was glad that I was now on this side of the ocean.

When the sun set, we walked on the boardwalk, where we ate pizza and climbed onto the rides. We rode helicopters, fire trucks, a Ferris wheel, and horses that went up and down on the carousel. I remember how high those wooden horses seemed. At first Papa would stand by my side to keep me safe. I think it was while on that carousel that I knew I once more had a father to protect me.

Toward the end of the summer Mama took us to a farmers' market to buy fabric to make new curtains for our bedroom. Papa had given each of us two dollars to spend however we chose. We passed a stall that sold movies.

"Let's see what they have here. Hmm, how would you girls like to pick a movie to watch at home?" Mama asked as she browsed through the piles of videos that cost only ninety-nine cents each.

Suddenly my eyes lit up. "Mama, look! I think this is a ballet movie," I said in my heavily accented English. I no longer spoke Krio, not even to my sister, because Mama had promised to sign me up for ballet lessons as soon as I could understand and speak English.

Mama took the box from my hand to examine it. "Michaela, what a clever little girl you are! This is the Balanchine *Nutcracker*, performed by the New York City Ballet!"

She handed it back to me, and I twirled around on my toes. I was happy to have this ballet movie, especially because we had lost a piece of luggage on our return trip from Africa. I no longer had the picture of the ballerina, which had been such an important part of my life in Africa. I proudly handed one of my dollar bills to the cashier to pay for *The Nutcracker*.

Later that day, while Mama sewed the new curtains for our bedroom, Mia and I watched *The Nutcracker* over and over again. I took it to bed with me that night and played it again the next morning and every day afterward. Mia and I would dance along to it in our family room.

What I had only been able to imagine when I first looked at the magazine picture of the ballerina had now become reality. Soon I was begging for those ballet lessons that Mama had promised me in the hotel room in Ghana. Mama hung a calendar on the wall of our bedroom and circled the date September 13, 1999. Then she wrote, "Ballet Lessons" in red ink, and I was over the moon with joy.

·•· *Chapter 13* ·•·

BABY EMMA

From morning until bedtime, my new life as Michaela was totally different from my life as Mabinty. I would awake in a soft bed, snuggled under a cozy comforter with a rainbow on it. Then I would hurry downstairs to the bright, cheerful kitchen, where my mother, who would be reading at the kitchen table, would greet me with a smile and a warm hug.

I loved opening the kitchen cabinet to choose my cereal for breakfast. I would pour it into a bright yellow bowl and add a scoop of fruit, either strawberries, blueberries, or raspberries. Then I'd pour in a cup of milk. Having so many choices made me feel giddy with joy. Best of all, I could eat until my belly was full. I didn't have to wait until someone filled the bowls for twenty-six other children.

When I needed to use the toilet, I could just jump up and run to the bathroom. I didn't have to worry about someone stealing my food if I left it behind. I flushed without fear of falling into a pit of smelly waste. Then I washed my hands with a foamy pink soap that squirted from a bottle. Ah yes, in America everything smelled good, I thought, even the toilet!

There were lights everywhere in my new home. At first Mia and I would run around, flicking them on and off. There were so many switches to so many things, like the machines that churned and whined all over the house. There were big, noisy machines for cleaning. One machine washed the clothes, a second machine dried the clothes, and a third machine washed the dishes. There was even a machine for sucking the crumbs and dirt from the floors.

Mama didn't have to light the wood fire to cook rice. In my new house she cooked on a stove with a hot top, but no flames. "Where is the fire?" I asked the first time I watched her cook.

"It runs with electricity," Mama explained as she slid a pan of cookies into the oven. I flicked on the light in the oven to watch in wonderment as the cookies gradually turned crispy and golden.

After breakfast Mia and I would choose something to wear. We had a closet full of colorful dresses. We would giggle and chatter away as we debated whether to wear pink, purple, polka dots, or prints. We always chose matching outfits, and people often thought we were twins.

Our parents encouraged us to try a different kind of food every day so that we could get used to eating new foods. In Sierra Leone all that we had ever eaten was rice, pepper, mealie meal, cassava, mango, and banana. Now Mama and Papa wanted us to taste corn, peas, carrots, applesauce, and many other strange foods. Mia and I liked "tinky-winks" best. Everyone else called them buffalo wings, but that was such a long name to learn. After a while even the waitresses in the nearby diner ended up calling them tinky-winks, and they called us their favorite girls.

In America no one teased me and no one abused me. Unlike Auntie Fatmata, my new mama and papa didn't use a switch to punish me. Instead they used a time-out chair, where I would be forced to sit still and be quiet for three minutes when I couldn't behave.

Mama made a list of rules to help us learn better behavior. She hung it on the door. Several times a day she would say, "Let's read our rules." We were so excited about reading English that we gladly read the rules aloud:

RULES
1. No hit.
2. No bite.

3. No pinch.
4. No scratch.
5. No say caca.

Soon we were no longer hitting, biting, pinching, scratching, or using potty language. The only things we continued to abuse were our baby dolls. We would beat them and shout at them, shaking them until their heads nearly fell off, mimicking the way Auntie Fatmata had treated the children in the orphanage.

We had been with our new family for two months when, one day, our adoption social worker called Mama with a problem. She had a birth mother who wasn't sure whether she wanted to keep her baby or put her up for adoption, and she needed a week or so to make the decision. The social worker wondered if Mama and Papa would be willing to care for the newborn baby for a week. Mama said yes, and Baby Emma came to live with us for a short while.

Mama would wheel Baby Emma's carriage from room to room so that she'd never be alone. She would pick up Emma and rock her in the rocking chair. Mia and I would sit on the floor in front of her, holding our dolls as we watched her care for the tiny infant.

She would say to us, "A good mama hugs her baby gently. A good mama doesn't hit her baby. A good mama says nice words to her baby and rubs her back. A good

mama kisses her baby and lets her know she is loved."
By the end of the week Mia and I knew that Auntie Fatmata's way was not the right way to care for babies.

On the day that the social worker picked up Baby Emma to bring her home to her birth mother, Mama let us each hold her for a few minutes. She took pictures of us with her. In my picture I am kissing Baby Emma's head so that she will know she is loved.

Our mama and papa took us on a vacation to Vermont the day after Baby Emma left so that we wouldn't miss her too much. But we missed her anyway and talked about her the whole trip. Two months later Santa Claus brought us each a doll that looked exactly like Baby Emma. We each named our new doll Baby Emma, and we practiced taking good care of our babies, just as Mama had taken care of the real Baby Emma. Between our list of rules and Baby Emma's visit, Mia and I learned to become gentle in our play. Neither of us ever struck each other or another child after that.

Chapter 14

INTO THE WORLD OF BALLET

Though no one made fun of my spots in America, sometimes a child would point at me and ask his parent, "What's wrong with that little girl?" Then I would want to crawl into a hole and disappear. If we were far enough away from the child, we just walked away as though we didn't hear him. Sometimes we were standing so close that we couldn't ignore him. Then Mama would explain vitiligo, and eventually I learned to do that too, because Mama said, "Sometimes it's better to answer the child's question so that he'll understand there's nothing at all wrong with you. Sometimes kids are just being curious, not mean."

When it came time for my first ballet lesson, I dreaded wearing a leotard. We had visited the dance studio on the day that Mama registered Mia and me. There I discovered that we would be facing a mirror the entire time. I hated the idea of staring at my spots in the mirror through a lesson, so when we went shopping for dance wear, I insisted on a turtlenecked, long-sleeved leotard.

Mia and I tried on our new leotards, tights, and ballet slippers the second we arrived home. I turned on the *Nutcracker* videotape, and we danced for hours in the family room. I was squirming, scratching, and dripping with sweat while we danced, but Mia was comfortable in her cap-sleeved leotard.

That evening over dinner Mia told our father all about our dance-wear purchases. I sat sulking while she described her new pink leotard. "Michaela, what's wrong?" Papa asked.

"My leotard is hot. It makes me itch," I complained.

"Does your leotard make you itch too?" he asked Mia.

"Of course not. Mine has short sleeves and a neck like this," she answered, drawing a U on her chest.

"Is your leotard different?" Papa asked me.

Tears pooled in my eyes, and I said, "Yes, mine has long sleeves and a turtleneck."

"Why did Mama choose a different leotard for you?"

"She didn't choose it. I did. I chose it so that I couldn't see my spots in the mirror," I answered, feeling very much like Number Twenty-Seven again as I swiped at the tears that now dripped down my cheeks.

"Oh, sweetie, you won't need to wear that hot leotard," Mama said. "I bought a second one just like Mia's, in case you changed your mind."

"But the kids will see my spots, and I'll see them in the mirror," I said, feeling sorry for myself.

Mama wasn't into self-pity. She said to me, "Well, sweetie, you won't be able to wear a long-sleeved leotard with a turtleneck when you're a world-famous ballerina, so you might as well get used to not wearing one now."

Though I was usually stubborn, for once I took her advice without argument. The next day I went off to ballet class wearing the pink cap-sleeved leotard with the low neckline.

When I walked into dance class with Mia and ten other little girls, my expectations were high. I had already memorized the choreography of the Balanchine *Nutcracker,* so I expected to come out of class dancing like a real ballerina. Much to my disappointment, only one half of the session was ballet, and the other half was tap. I had nothing against tap, but I wanted the whole session to be ballet.

We learned the five basic positions, and how to plié and tendu. I expected us to immediately move on to greater things, like arabesques, grands jetés, and pirouettes, but we couldn't. Two of the little girls cried for their parents, and the teachers took time to calm them down. Then some of the girls couldn't seem to get the dance steps quite right. Too soon the ballet half of class was done, and we were instructed to put on our tap shoes. Once the teachers finished tying the ribbons on our tap shoes, class was almost over.

When we came out of our lesson, Mia cheerfully skipped over to our mother and said, "Mama, I just loved dance class!"

Mama took one look at my stormy face and didn't say a word to me until we got to the car. Then she asked, "What's wrong, Michaela?"

"I hated it. They didn't teach enough ballet. I wanted to pirouette."

Mama explained that dancing ballet was like reading a book. "First you learn the letters. Then you learn the words. Finally you put the words together to make a story. You need to learn the simple steps, like tendu, before you can dance a full ballet.

"Let's give it another week or so, and see if it improves. If you don't like it any better, I'll find you a different dance class," she promised.

That afternoon Mia and I showed Mama what we had learned. Then we ran off and watched *The Nutcracker*. First we danced the party scene, and then we danced "Waltz of the Flowers."

"Now *this* is what I mean by dancing," I said as I danced

the role of Dewdrop, tippy-toeing around Mia and the dolls I had arranged on the floor as Flowers.

The following week I went to dance class thinking that we would progress to real dancing. We went over the same steps that we had learned before. Before we could learn a new step, it was time for tap. By the third class I had learned to tell time. Now I noticed that we spent only twenty minutes on ballet, and forty minutes on tap.

I stuck with that class for several more weeks, but the time we spent on ballet grew shorter as the time we spent on tap grew longer. "Mama, I'm learning too much tap. I'm afraid I'll never learn to be a ballerina here," I whispered into my mother's ear one afternoon after class.

At Christmastime Papa bought us tickets to see the nearby Pennsylvania Ballet dance *The Nutcracker.* Mama had sewn red velvet dresses with white eyelet pinafores for Mia and me. We wore those dresses with green ribbons in our hair and black patent-leather dress shoes on our feet. We looked like the Party Children in *The Nutcracker.*

When we entered the lobby of the Academy of Music in Philadelphia, my heart skipped a beat: the Sugar Plum Fairy was seated there, and children were lined up to have their pictures taken with her. Mia and I lined up too, and I decided at that moment that I would one day dance the role of the Sugar Plum Fairy.

The performance was breathtaking. I sat spellbound,

watching every step and every movement of the dancers' arms and heads. After the ballet Papa said, "What did you think about that, girls?"

I said, "It was nearly perfect!"

"Nearly? Why nearly?" he asked.

"Because in the snow scene, one of the dancers raised the wrong arm and stepped on the wrong foot," I answered. "I'd like to see it again tomorrow. Maybe then it will be perfect."

My parents laughed. "Just one *Nutcracker* a year," Papa said.

"But we'll see a different ballet later in the season," Mama promised.

Over dinner Mama asked, "What role would you like to dance, if you could?"

"Soon I'd like to dance the role of a Party Girl or Marie, but when I get bigger I want to dance the Arabian and the Sugar Plum Fairy," I answered.

"What about you, Mia? What was your favorite part?" Papa asked.

"I liked the orchestra best," my sister answered. "I liked that black instrument with the silver keys and the pointy top. That one played a note, and everybody else followed. What was it?"

"The oboe? You watched the oboist the entire time?" Mama asked.

"Not the entire time. I watched the dancers some of

the time, but I always listened for that instrument with the pointy top . . . the oboe," Mia explained.

That night Mia and I talked about *The Nutcracker* until late into the night. We were so excited that we had difficulty sleeping. When I finally did, I dreamt of dancing on the stage at the Academy of Music.

Just days before my fifth birthday, my mother took me to Philadelphia to register me for ballet lessons at the Rock School for Dance Education. Mia came with us, but she didn't sign up for class. "I like tap dancing. I don't want to change dance schools."

When I was introduced to the director of the school, I raised my leg straight up into the air and held it there. "See what I can do? I want to learn to do even more," I said. The director laughed and put me into Pre-Ballet 2.

My new dance class at the Rock School was so much more fun than the class I had been taking. My teacher made it interesting. He taught us real ballet steps and let us make up our own combinations. Best of all, we didn't have to stop to put on tap shoes.

At the end of the semester the Rock School would be performing a showcase at the Academy of Music, the same place where I had seen *The Nutcracker.* We were rehearsing for the showcase when our ballet teacher had us join hands to form a circle. As I reached out to link my hand with the girl beside me, she pressed her hand to her mouth and looked at me with horror. She then whispered to the girl beside her and pointed to my neck and chest.

I felt like Number Twenty-Seven all over again. I looked across the room at my reflection in the mirror. *You are one ugly girl*, I told myself, but at that very moment, Nora, the oldest and best dancer in the class, crossed the room toward me. Then, raising her hand, she said to the teacher, "May I dance next to Michaela? She's my best friend."

Nora stood beside me and squeezed my hand, whispering, "You're a good dancer for such a little kid." I was thrilled. Nora was the one who was good. She had been dancing ballet for three years, and I admired her. I just could not believe that she would single me out for attention. For the rest of the year I stood directly behind her in class and mimicked every movement that she made.

The day of the showcase finally arrived. As Mama walked me into the Academy of Music, I tugged at her hand. She leaned over, and I whispered into her ear. "Please notice if you can see my spots from the audience. If you can't, then I know that I can be a professional ballerina someday." But when I walked onto the stage, all of my worries flew from my mind. I was just thrilled to be dancing on such a grand stage.

When the audience applauded, I felt a rush. It was

such an intoxicating feeling that I knew I could not live without it. I realized then that I just had to become a professional ballerina.

During intermission I threw myself into Mama's arms and asked, "Well, did you see them?"

"No . . . not at all," Mama whispered, like a conspirator. "It was like magic. From a distance they looked like a sprinkling of pixie dust or glitter."

I sighed and said, "Now I know that I will be a professional ballerina."

It took me years to realize that my mother had lied to me that evening, but it was a good lie. At that point in my life I needed to believe that my hated spots looked like magical pixie dust and would not stand in the way of my dream.

·•· *Chapter 15* ·•·

A New Sister

Our childhood in Africa had been different from that of most American kids, so it took Mia and me a while to get used to playing with them. I thought it was very funny when snack time rolled around and one of my kindergarten friends exclaimed, "Finally! I'm starving!" I looked at all the plump arms and legs, and knew that no one in my class was starving.

One day during recess the boys were playing with sticks and pretending that they were guns. Eddie, the biggest kid in our class, shot at Todd and said, "Bang, bang! You're dead."

Todd fell to the ground, folded his hands neatly on his chest, and closed his eyes.

"Look, Todd's dead," Eddie said.

I walked over to Todd and looked down at him. I rolled my eyes. "Todd's not dead," I scoffed.

"Yes, he is," Eddie argued.

"Mia, come here and look. Is Todd dead?" I asked.

Mia looked down at Todd and giggled. "Of course Todd's not dead."

By now all of the other kids had gathered around us to listen to our argument. "How do you know that Todd's not dead?" one of the girls asked me.

"Because I've seen a lot of dead people, and that's not what a dead person looks like."

"Well, what does a dead person look like?" Eddie asked.

"I'll show you," I answered. I lay down on the ground, opened my eyes wide, and let my mouth fall open.

"That's exactly what a dead person looks like," Mia confirmed as she looked down at me. Both she and I gained a certain degree of respect from our peers because we knew what dead people looked like.

The following year I started to take ballet and other types of dance at a school closer to my home in New Jersey. Though I had a passion for ballet, I now found that I loved all kinds of dancing. Mia and I had a great time taking jazz and tap together. Yet no matter how much fun I had in those classes, ballet was my first love. I couldn't live without it.

Suzanne Slenn, my ballet teacher, said, "You were

fortunate to have been born with naturally great extension and talent. I expect more of you because of that." So I worked very hard to please her.

I didn't have very good control of my extension in those days. While other children were having their parents or their dentists pull out their baby teeth, I was knocking mine out with my feet when I did grands battements.

One afternoon, when my mother was at the supermarket next door to the dance school, I ran out of ballet class with blood pouring out of my mouth. My friend Samantha's mother helped me wash the blood off my face and leotard. She comforted me by telling me that I had kicks so high that even a Rockette would envy them.

Right around the time my teeth were coming out, two other important things happened to me . . . and to my family. We got a new sister, and we began homeschooling.

One afternoon we got a call out of the blue from the adoptive mother of Isatu Bangura, another girl from our orphanage. Isatu had been called Number Two by the aunties because they loved her. Mia and I loved her too and stayed in touch with her in America, but Isatu's adoption wasn't working out.

When the telephone rang, we were sitting at the kitchen table planning a trip to Scotland to celebrate my parents' wedding anniversary. My mother excused herself from our planning to take the phone call upstairs.

About half an hour later, Mama came down and asked Papa, "Can we take Isatu?"

Papa said, "Of course not!"

Mama looked stunned. "But why not?" she asked.

"Isatu's not our child. Do you know how complicated it would be to take someone else's child to a foreign country?" my father asked.

"Oh, please, please . . . can Isatu come to Scotland too?" Mia and I chimed in.

"Oh, I don't mean take her to Scotland," Mama said. "I mean can we adopt her? Her American mother isn't able to keep her, and I'd hate to see her have to go into foster care."

Papa laughed. "I thought you wanted to take her to Scotland with us. Of course we can adopt her!" That's my father. He always sweats the small stuff, like what kind of cereal to buy at the supermarket, but when it comes to the big, momentous decisions like adoption, he responds immediately with an open and generous heart. Mia and I were so happy. We hugged our parents and planned for our new sister to arrive.

On Isatu's first night with us I lay awake thinking about how strange fate is. Here Mia and I were, Number Twenty-Six and Number Twenty-Seven, the two least favored children from the orphanage, and we were now beloved by our mama and papa. Isatu, on the other hand, had been a favorite of the aunties as Number Two, but her situation was reversed when she arrived in America. I could make no sense of this, but felt immensely thankful for where fate had landed me.

Soon after Isatu arrived, she said, "It's not fair. Mia and Michaela are *M* names, but I have an *I* name." I suggested that she change her name to something more exotic, like Svetlana, Tatiana, or Natalia, names of Russia's most famous ballerinas. But Isatu said, "No, I want an *M* name." So she became Mariel.

We began homeschooling when Papa started working for a Japanese company. His work hours changed so that they would overlap with the working day in Japan. This meant that he left for work later in the morning, but he also came home much later at night. Mia, Mariel, and I missed spending time with our papa. He used to read to us every night, but now we saw him only in the mornings and on weekends.

One night I missed Papa so much that I lay awake until I heard him come home. Then I tiptoed down the stairs and threw myself into his arms. "Papa! I miss you!" I cried out.

"I miss you too," he said as he held me in a bear hug.

He said to Mama, "I adopted these three little girls, but I hardly ever get a chance to see my princesses."

The next morning Mama said, "Would you girls like to be homeschooled? Then you can wake up later and have breakfast with Papa. At night you can eat dinner late with Papa, and he can read you bedtime stories again." Because Mia, Mariel, and I were best friends as well as sisters, we liked the idea of having our own homeschool, so we happily said, "Yes!"

I'm glad that we agreed, because homeschool turned out to be fun. We were able to get all of our schoolwork done early enough to make it to our lessons and team practices on time. Best of all, we spent time with Papa when we got home.

Homeschooling also made it easier for me when I returned to the Rock School at the age of seven. I never had to worry about going to sleep late or waking up early in the mornings.

Because I was a little older and more experienced this time, I had to audition to see what level I'd be in that fall. I was hoping to get into Level 1 or possibly into Level 1X. I was totally shocked and thrilled when I was accepted into the Level 2 ballet class . . . the first pointe class.

I felt little pitter-patters in my heart the day I tried on my first pointe shoes. The satin felt exactly as I had thought it would when I found the photo of the ballerina on the magazine. As I held the barre in the pointe-shoe store, I rolled up onto the tips of my toes, as my teacher had taught us. Suddenly I felt taller and more elegant. I removed my hand from the barre and balanced en pointe for the first time in my life. I felt so happy that I almost cried! I couldn't believe that, the very next day, I would dance in class en pointe. That night I rubbed the satin of my new pointe shoes with my fingers as I fell asleep, dreaming of becoming a real ballerina.

·•· *Chapter 16* ·•·

THE CANNED-FOOD BIRTHDAY

Mia, Mariel, and I were the same age. With our short haircuts, long legs, and deep chocolate skin, we passed for triplets. Though this was fun for us, it sometimes created a lot of confusion. When we joined the swim team at our community center, our names were usually listed on the meet sheets by first initial, last name, so we were each M. DePrince. At meets each swimmer was only allowed to swim three events. At one meet I overheard a boy from another team complaining to his mother, "It just isn't fair! Why can I only swim three times? I've seen M. DePrince swim nine times!"

We were a busy threesome. Besides going to swim team practice, we took dance and music lessons. Though we swam on the same team, we were always in different dance classes and we played different musical instruments. We never felt lonely being homeschooled, because we had each other, and friends from our swim team and dance classes.

One night, shortly before my eighth birthday, I watched the news on television with my brother Teddy and learned that the local food shelf was running out of food.

"What's a food shelf?" I asked Teddy.

"It's a place that people go to get free food, if they've run out of money."

I had never before thought that people might be hungry in America. This shocked me. I asked, "What kind of food does the food shelf need?"

"Oh, I suppose it needs canned goods, like peas, corn, beans, carrots, spaghetti. . . . Why, Monkey, are you planning to donate canned goods?"

I wrapped my arms around Teddy's neck and asked, "If I do that, will you help me?"

"Sure, you know I would," he answered.

The next afternoon, when my mother, my sisters, and I were baking holiday cookies, I asked, "Mama, can I have a birthday party?"

"Of course, sweetie," she answered. After she slid the cookie sheets into the oven, she washed her hands, grabbed a pen and a pad of paper from a kitchen drawer, and sat down at the table with me. "Whom do you want to invite?" she asked.

"Jamie, Tabrea, Sabrina, Lauren, Briana, Katie, Annie,

Rachel, Maria, Adriana, Jessica, Kaitlyn, Kristin . . ." On and on I went, until I had over thirty-five girls on the list.

"Wow! That's a lot of girls! What kind of a party were you thinking of having?" Mama asked me.

"Oh, I would love to have a real ball and wear a gown like Sleeping Beauty or Cinderella."

"What if the girls you're inviting don't own gowns?" she asked me.

"They can just wear special dresses, or they can borrow dresses from each other."

"Just think of all the gifts you'll get," Mariel said as she kneaded cookie dough at the kitchen counter, occasionally popping some raw dough into her mouth.

"Don't eat the raw dough!" I snapped, because I was irritated that she was adding her two cents to my party plans. "I don't want them to buy me gifts. All I want for my birthday is cans," I said.

"Cans?" my mother asked.

"Cans?" Mariel repeated.

"Cans, like cans of food?" Mia asked.

"Yep, cans . . . like cans of peas, cans of corn, cans of fruit. I want to donate cans to the food shelf. I heard on television that the food shelves that give food to the poor are running out of cans."

Mama liked my idea, but told me that she'd have to look into it. The next week she discovered that it cost only seventy-five dollars to rent a hall in a local hotel.

"And the birthday cake comes with that price!" she exclaimed.

When Teddy came over for dinner, I reminded him that he had promised to help me collect cans for the food shelf.

"Okay, I'll help. Just tell me what you want me to do," he said.

Teddy was a DJ, so I asked if he would DJ my party. He agreed, so on my birthday he and his girlfriend played music and taught all of my friends the hokey-pokey, the electric slide, cotton-eyed Joe, and other fun dances. Teddy's hair was dyed blue that night. My friends all thought that he was cute and supercool. That made me feel so proud of him. It was like having a celebrity for a big brother.

I wore a burgundy A-line gown with gold sparkles on the top. Papa said that I looked beautiful, and my sisters and friends looked beautiful in their dresses too. We all felt as if we were Hollywood stars going to the Academy Awards. The *Philadelphia Inquirer* even sent a reporter and photographer to cover the event, just as if it was a big social affair.

That night, after the party, Adam helped Mia and me weigh each bag of groceries on our scale. After I added up the pounds, I learned that I had received 1,824 pounds of canned goods for my birthday. That was nearly a ton of food! Adam and my mama helped us take all of the groceries to a food shelf in Camden, New Jersey. As we talked to the woman in charge of the food shelf and she told us about the many families that would use our canned food, I realized that giving something on my birthday felt a lot better than getting gifts. It was a feeling that I've never forgotten.

·•· *Chapter 17* ·•·

FEARS

Life was good for me in America. I had pretty clothes, plenty to eat, and lots of love. My family took fun vacations to the beach, Arizona, and even Walt Disney World. Best of all, I danced. I would have liked to leave all of my bad memories and heartbreak behind in Sierra Leone, but I didn't. I had frequent nightmares. In one dream my African mama was being chased by debils and struggled to escape them, but I held her back. I was too small to run fast. When the debils caught us, I'd wake up panicked and sweating. In another dream I managed to save Teacher Sarah, but when I woke up I'd remember that I hadn't.

My sisters and I had many of the same fears, and they lingered for a long time. We were terrified of monkeys.

To us they were not cute or cuddly animals, like Curious George. In Africa they often stole mangoes and bananas from the trees. We needed those fruits, especially when we ran out of other food. The monkeys even tried to steal mealie meal, cassava, or rice from our bowls. Because the squirrels in our front yard looked like monkeys, we were afraid of them too.

Dogs also scared us. Our family's dog, Alaska, had died of old age soon after we arrived in the United States so we didn't get to know him well. When Mama took us shopping in the local mall, she'd take us to the pet shop so we'd get used to small animals. As long as the puppies were in their cages, we loved watching them.

One summer day Adam took us to the mall. As usual we begged for a visit to the pet shop. We were admiring a cute little spotted puppy with floppy ears, when, without warning, the salesperson let it out of the cage so we could pet it.

We were wearing sandals, and the puppy began to yip and nip at our toes. Mia and I panicked. We took off together, running and screaming through the mall with our brother chasing us.

"Stop! Stop! Come back!" Adam shouted, but we kept going, afraid that the puppy was still chasing us.

When we finally turned back, we saw the police arresting Adam.

"Uh-oh! Adam's getting arrested," Mia said.

"What happened?" I asked.

"I dunno, but we'd better go back and save him," she advised.

One of the police officers came up to us. "Are you little girls all right?" he asked us.

We weren't about to talk to a strange man. I remember standing there trembling until a policewoman came over and asked the same question. I felt more comfortable answering her when she asked, "Where is your mother?"

"She's home," I said.

"Are you girls here all by yourselves?" she asked.

"No, we're with our big brother," Mia answered.

"Well, where is he?" she asked.

I pointed in Adam's direction. "He's right there."

"But the dog bit our toes, so we ran away from him," Mia explained.

"From your brother?" the police officer asked.

"No, from the dog," I said.

The policewoman brought us to Adam. "Do you know this man?" she asked.

"Of course," I answered. "That's Adam. He's our big brother."

Mia wrapped her arms around Adam and begged him to take us to the food court, but he didn't. He took us right home. When he got there, he said to our mother, "I will never, ever take them out in public again." He did eventually take us out, but first we had to promise never to run away from him again.

We were still learning English and we didn't have a full vocabulary, so it was hard to explain to our family why we were so afraid of dogs. But one day, as I watched my papa shave, I figured out how to say it. My father had foamy white shaving cream on his face, and I said, "You look like the mad dog that came to our orphanage one day."

Papa didn't understand, so I took his can of shaving cream and squirted some onto my chin. Then I dropped to my hands and knees, growling and snapping my teeth as I showed him what had happened when a dog growled at a group of us as we played soccer in the orphanage yard.

"Rabies!" Papa exclaimed. "No wonder you girls are so afraid of dogs."

Fireworks also frightened us. On our first Fourth of July in the United States, Papa and Mama took us to watch the fireworks. We didn't know what fireworks were, so Mama drew us each a picture of them and sprinkled glitter on them.

Mia and I carried our pictures to the field where we were going to watch the fireworks. When it was dark,

Papa pointed to the sky. I looked up, expecting to see glitter. What a shock it was to hear an explosion and see the real fireworks. "Bombs! Bombs!" Mia and I screamed. I thought the war had followed us to America.

Eventually I stopped being afraid of squirrels, puppies, and fireworks, but I was still afraid of humans. Nothing terrified me as much as the debils, who left mutilated bodies on the sides of the roads in my home country. In those early days of living in the United States, I saw debils everywhere, especially in the windows at night.

"Debils! Debils!" we screamed in those first nights in our new home, when we saw what were our own reflections or the reflections of our family members in our bedroom windows. I soon learned that there were no debils outside our second-story bedroom windows. But even today I don't like bare windows at night. I still feel the need to close my blinds tightly after dark.

Mia, Mariel, and I also hated camouflage clothing. We were convinced that every man who wore camouflage clothing was a debil. Once we were so terrified of a group of soldiers from nearby Fort Dix that we ran across a parking lot and into a highway. The soldiers chased us and rounded us up. I thought that they were going to kill us, but instead they turned us over to our mother.

Another time our fear of camouflage ruined what could have been the perfect ending to a day of ballet. Mama and Papa had taken us to New York City to see the ballet. After the performance we took too long to get to the coat check, and it was closed. Albert Evans, a principal dancer with the New York City Ballet, came to our rescue. He led us around the building in search of our coats. On the elevator he tried to strike up a conversation, but we were too terrified of him. Though I longed to talk to this famous ballet dancer, I didn't dare. He was wearing a blue camouflage parka, so I was convinced that he was a debil as well as a dancer. It upset me to think that a person who danced ballet might also kill me.

To this day I am also afraid of loud male voices. The debils were loud, whether they were shouting in anger or laughing in victory. Many times Mia, Mariel, and I would run into the house and report to our parents that there was an African man outside. It wouldn't matter what color he was. A shouting man was a debil.

Cheering fathers at a swim meet terrified me. Schoolteachers, ballet teachers, men on the street . . . whether they were of European, African, Asian, Native American, or Hispanic descent, it didn't matter. If I heard men shouting, I remembered the frightening voices of the debils on a rampage in my native Sierra Leone.

•→ Chapter 18 →•

BIGOTRY AND JEALOUSY

At first I thought that nothing could be more wonderful than my life in the United States. My family loved me. My sisters and I got along well. I had friends. I had lots of fun dancing, playing, and swimming. I believed that everything and everybody in this wonderful new country of mine was perfect. Though my parents and brothers were white, and my sisters and I were black, we didn't seem to care about skin color. It never occurred to me that we should feel any other way, and I never suspected that anyone else would care. I didn't know anything about racial intolerance then, but I learned about it soon enough. I felt very sad when I experienced it in my neighborhood, in restaurants, and in stores. But I felt worse when I discovered it in the world of ballet.

My earliest experience of bigotry occurred in my own front yard. Mia and I were dressed in hand-me-down gowns, having a tea party on the lawn with our dolls, when a neighbor walked over and said, "You girls will need to take your things and move your tea party out of sight of *my property*. I'm trying to sell my house. Someone is coming to look at it, and I don't want them to see the two of *you*."

At the time I didn't understand that there was racial prejudice in America, so I was confused about why the neighbor didn't want anyone to see us. "Are we ugly? Are we bad? Do we have grass stains on our clothes? Are we making too much noise?" Mia and I asked ourselves those questions, and many more.

Not long after the neighbor asked us to move off our lawn, we had another experience almost like the first. While at the mall, Mia and I skipped ahead of our mother. Two white women passed us and said, "Tsk, look at them, running around loose in the mall like a couple of wild animals."

Mia, Mariel, and I heard many comments like this when we were little, and they hurt our feelings because we took them to heart.

Then, one afternoon, Mama and Papa stopped at the video store and bought us the Disney movie *Ruby Bridges*. It was the story of how six-year-old Ruby Bridges led the crusade to integrate the schools in New Orleans. We watched it and were amazed by the idea of bigotry.

We talked about that movie with our parents afterward. And it helped me understand that the discrimination we experienced had nothing to do with whether we were pretty or not, or whether we made noise or had grass stains on our clothes. We could have been the most perfect children in the neighborhood, but some people would still have hated us for the color of our skin.

Ruby Bridges prepared us for an imperfect future. Now we understood why salesclerks in stores followed closely behind us and hovered over us while we shopped for clothes. We knew why they sometimes grabbed the clothes from our hands when we touched them. Once, when we were shopping for jeans, a white salesclerk told us to go shop where we belonged. Thanks to *Ruby Bridges*, we were not shocked by her behavior.

This is not to say that all of our encounters with white people were tainted with prejudice. The movie taught us that there were many white people who were like our parents. They were not filled with hatred.

When Ruby Bridges's father lost his job, a white neighbor offered him another one. The teacher who volunteered to teach Ruby Bridges was a white woman. Some of the white people in her neighborhood even walked behind the federal marshal's car when Ruby went to school.

• ◆ •

Even though I understand the reason why it happens, I still feel uncomfortable in stores and restaurants when people stare at our family. We had been with our parents a month or so when I began to forget that they were a different color than I was. When I looked at their faces, I just saw Mama and Papa. However, when other people stared at us, I'd remember that we were different. It bothered me then and bothers me even more now when people make me feel this way.

Today I can almost see the wheels turning in people's heads as they try to figure out why two white senior citizens are with a group of black teens. Recently, when Mia and I were shopping with Mama, I had my arm over Mama's shoulder as she was opening her purse to give Mia her credit card. A white man came up to her and said, "Ma'am, are you okay?"

It wasn't just white people who stared at us; it was black people as well. It wasn't just white people who showed us how racist they were. Black people often did that too.

Black women sometimes came up to Mama and told her that she wasn't raising us right because we didn't have hair extensions or straight parts in our hair. They sometimes criticized our parents because we had ashy skin from swimming in a chlorinated pool. Once a lady asked my mother, "What crazy social worker placed those girls with you?"

Papa thought it was funny that most of our experiences

with racism happened in the parking lot of our supermarket, and usually involved women. He would make a joke of it. Before he'd let us out of the car in the parking lot, he would ask us, "Did you lotion your arms and legs? Did you pick your hair? We don't want the nappy-hair-and-ashy-skin policewomen after us." We'd giggle and think Papa was very funny, but we also knew what would await us if we weren't perfectly groomed, so we'd reach for the lotion and hair picks that Mama always left in the car.

Despite the clowning around, both my mother and my father took the racism seriously. They warned us that we would be judged more harshly than little white girls in everything that we did; all of our failures would be blamed on race. We believed them, so we worked hard.

As we grew older, my sisters and I began to notice reports of racism in the newspapers, and they definitely changed the way we lived our lives. When I lived in Vermont, there were so many articles about the profiling of black drivers there that I was afraid to get my driver's license. Also, in Vermont supermarkets, when my mother wanted to use her credit card, the cashier never asked for her ID when she was alone or with my father. If she was with me or one of my sisters, the cashier would always ask to see her ID.

While living in New York City, we read reports of racial profiling in upscale stores, even reports of warrantless searches and pat-downs of black shoppers. As a result, I am always very careful of my every move in those stores.

I noticed a unique type of racial distrust in the city. My mother and I must look as if we know where we are going in Manhattan, because people always stop us and ask for directions. Even if she and I are linked arm in arm, when a white person needs directions, she will always ask my mother for them. If a black person needs directions, she will always ask me.

When I'm with either one of my parents, since they're now senior citizens, I'm often assumed to be their home health aide. When I use the laundry room in our apartment complex, the nannies will talk to me but they will never talk to my parents. The same thing happens with the white residents in the building, only in reverse. They'll talk to my parents but not to me.

Sometimes an incident of bigotry might even be funny. My most humorous encounters are a result of stereotyping. Often, upon learning that I am a dancer, someone will ask me, "What kind of dancing do you do . . . hip-hop?" This makes my ballerina friends laugh. We all look alike: lean, long-legged, hair in buns, and because of the rotation of our hips, our toes point out like ducks'. Why are they presumed to be ballerinas, but I am presumed to be a hip-hop artist?

Now that I'm older, I've learned to detach my personal feelings from the bigotry. I'm able to step back and look at it for what it is: a combination of fear and ignorance. Unless I'm in physical danger or my civil rights are being violated, I ignore it. I tell myself that it isn't worth getting worked up about. However, there is one form of racial discrimination that I am unable to ignore, and that is the racial bias in the world of ballet.

Chapter 19

WHERE ARE THE BLACK BALLERINAS?

I first recognized that there is racial inequality in ballet when I was only four years old and had watched that first video of *The Nutcracker.* I couldn't put it into complicated language at the time. I didn't know the words *bigotry, prejudice,* or *discrimination.* I was only able to ask, "Mama, where are the black ballerinas?"

When my parents took me to see the Pennsylvania Ballet's *Nutcracker,* I was happy to see not one, but two black ballerinas that day: Nikkia Parish and Heidi Cruz.

I noticed Meredith Rainey, a black male dancer, there too, and I would eventually learn that black male ballet dancers are not so rare.

By the time I was eight years old, my parents had taken Mia, Mariel, and me to see ballet in New York City as well as Philadelphia. I had seen performances by Philadanco!, the Pennsylvania Ballet, the American Ballet Theatre, and the Alvin Ailey American Dance Theater. By then I had been taking dance lessons for three years and understood the differences between dance styles.

I began peppering my parents with questions that they couldn't answer, such as "Why are there lots of black dancers in the contemporary companies, but not in the classical and neoclassical companies that tell the stories that I love so much?"

My mother promised to take me to see a neoclassical company that had many black ballerinas. "It's the Dance Theatre of Harlem," she said, "and it features the type of story ballets that you love." I remember leaning over her shoulder, charged with excitement as she went online to buy tickets, and the disappointment that I felt when Mama said, "Oh no! It closed! Look, it says right here that the Dance Theatre of Harlem's professional company is no longer performing, because it lacks the money to continue."

I felt a lump in my throat. "Mama, where can a black ballerina dance in a classical?" I asked, but my mother didn't have an answer to my question.

There were many black kids, girls and boys, who attended the Rock School with me in Philadelphia, and soon I began to wonder what would happen when we grew up, since there were hardly any black dancers in ballet companies. I decided that there had to be ballet

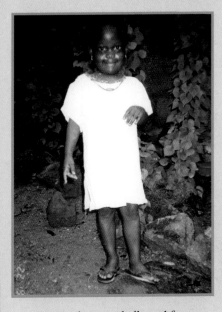

Despite having a belly and face swollen by malnutrition at age three and a half, I'm standing happy and proud because an American visitor just painted my fingernails.

This dress was a hand-me-down donation, but at the time, it was the prettiest dress I had ever seen. The grass mat beneath my feet is the sleeping mat that I shared with Mia.

The children from our orphanage at the safe house in Guinea
(I'm at the far left, in front of Mia).

After escaping Sierra Leone, we arrived at this bleak United Nations refugee camp in Guinea before moving to the safe house.

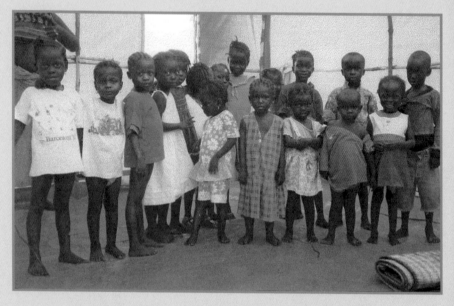

Inside the plastic hut at the refugee camp (I'm at the far left). When we got there, we were all hungry and covered with chicken pox.